DON'T BITCH
BITCH

JUST GET
RICH

DON'T BITCH

JUST GET RICH

Radically change your life forever

TONEY FITZGERALD
WITH THE HELP OF TERRY WALSH

SIMON & SCHUSTER

AUSTRALIA

This book is dedicated to my brother
Michael Fitzgerald who sadly passed away
on the 12th October 2005.
May his spirit forever be in our hearts

DON'T BITCH, JUST GET RICH
First published in Australia in 2006 by
Simon & Schuster (Australia) Pty Limited   .
Suite 2, Lower Ground Floor,
14–16 Suakin Street,
Pymble NSW 2073
A Viacom Company
Sydney New York London Toronto
Visit our website at www.simonsaysaustralia.com

© 2006 Toney Fitzgerald

Cataloguing-in-Publication data:

Fitzgerald, Toney.
Don't bitch, just get rich : radically change your life
forever.
Includes index.
ISBN 0 7318 1273 5.
1. Attitude change. 2. Self-actualization (Psychology).
3. Success. I. Title.
158.1

Cover design by Melissa Keogh
Typeset in 11 on 13.5 Sabon by Kirby Jones
Printed in Australia by Griffin Press
10 9 8 7 6 5 4 3 2 1

Contents

Acknowledgments

Throughout my life I have been blessed to share a connection with so many people who have supported me both personally and professionally. The cornerstone of the idea for *Don't Bitch Just Get Rich* was seeded in early 2003. Since then it has been an exciting journey, sometimes fraught but always challenging, and now finally we have arrived at the published book.

Along the road in crafting and shaping this book, I have been assisted by some truly extraordinary people. Firstly the most important and valuable person has been my main 'wing man' Terry Walsh, who has from day one been my co-creative partner and whose tremendous assistance has made this book a dream come true. I thank you for your amazing creative contribution, guidance and wisdom to make this book a reality. Without you this book would not exist as it is today.

I am also indebted to my family for believing in me and supporting my dreams, my father Colin, my mother Cecily, my brother Gary and my late brother Michael; his children Joshua, Rebecca and Katie and my Aunty Robyn Oliver. Thank you for your support.

I also would like to thank some of my great friends Philip and Jane Strachan; Guy Sampson; Di Hunter; Libby Selep; Belinda Selep; Denise Moser; Michelle Richmond, Collette Brodie; Sandy Ellison; Hans and Collet Jakobi; Claudia Boland; Karen McCreadie; Marianella Medrano Michelle Duval; Dave Pearce; Elisabeth Gortschacher; Miranda Barnes; Andy

Green; Adele Basheer; Steve Fanale; Lyndal Maloney; Debbie Verell; Annabel Marvel; Rachel Packer; Bronwyn Buck who have given me feedback on the first drafts and always listened to my raves and rants about the book.

A very special thank you to all the staff at Simon & Schuster Australia, especially Jon Attenborough (CEO) for believing in me and backing my second book, and Julia Collingwood for her tireless efforts in helping me to get the book over the finishing line.

Finally, to all my mentors, coaches and spiritual guides along my journey, thank you for helping me discover, shape and craft my talents so that I may inspire others to aspire to be the best they can be both personally and professionally.

The woods are lovely, dark and deep.
But I have promises to keep,
And miles to go before I sleep,
And miles to go before I sleep.

ROBERT FROST,
Stopping by Woods on a Snowy Evening

Introduction: Cards on the table

'John woke up one day and decided he would get rich. A year later he was rolling in it.' I would love to begin this book writing something like that, but no one would take me seriously. However, that is precisely what this book is about: waking up one morning, making an unconditional decision to get rich, and then doing it.

Getting rich is, without exaggeration, pretty simple. After all, money obeys fairly straightforward, well-defined rules, and wealth-creation strategies are not exactly nuclear physics; it's all mostly common sense.

Take, for example, the basic rule that you get rich by making more — lots more — than you spend. This is the first principle, the one all the other get-rich formulas are derived from, and there's nothing complicated in it, is there?

So why can't you, just like John, get out of bed one morning, make a decision to get rich and start from that day on to do precisely that? Why don't you use the get-rich formulas you already know? Why don't you set down your goals in dollar figures and go for them? Why have you read 25 get-rich books, diligently completed 16 courses on the paths to success, listened enthusiastically to umpteen motivational speakers churn out the same obvious truths again and again, and still not done anything?

Have you ever asked yourself questions like these? If you have, you're not alone.

Countless times during my years of lifestyle coaching, I have listened to the same plea for help: 'I know what to do, so why don't I do it? What is my problem?'

Actually, identifying the problem is the easy part. It's called inertia. The solution, on the other hand, is a little more complicated, and that is where this book will help you.

You are about to learn how to conquer inertia. Once it's beaten, there's nothing to stop you becoming unstoppable. I mean *really, really* unstoppable. Translated into dollars, that means getting rich. If you translate it into any of your other ambitions, it means getting what you *really, really* want in life.

Think about it for a minute. Wouldn't it be wonderful if you were unstoppable? What a joy life would be if nothing could come between you and your dreams! Imagine the happiness of achieving whatever you wanted to achieve in life, just because you said you would!

Imagine if your word had that sort of power! What couldn't you do?

Think ahead and hear yourself saying, 'I said I would and I did!' Wow! How rewarding would that be?

In all humility, and with gratitude to the many people who have inspired and instructed me, I believe I have discovered a way to become unstoppable. Finally, after years of searching, I have hit upon a solution to the problem of personal inertia.

And here is my promise to you, my reader: when you solve the problem of your own inertia, your life will change!

You are going to learn how to stop bitching about not getting what you want out of life and start getting it. Whether you want to enrich your life through more money or just want greater self-realisation, you will find this book both relevant and rewarding.

But a word of caution. What you are about to read is going to be challenging, because becoming unstoppable involves a radical, life-long, permanent change. It requires an uncompromising conversion. It's a personal turnaround, a transformation, and for some, a long overdue wake-up call.

In the book we call this conversion *metanoia*, which we define as a radical change of mind-set, a total personal revolution that produces a new way of thinking and believing. To bring this about — to break through the inertia barrier — I will teach you, step by step, about an extraordinary source of personal power. I have named it 'the empowering promise'; a phrase that, believe me, you will never forget.

If you make the empowering promise, fully understanding its profound consequences — both disruptive and transformative — you will be on your way to becoming unstoppable. If it's money you want, you will get it; if it's the simple, ordinary happiness of living the life that is really you, that, too, will be yours.

Why? What's so special about the empowering promise? Why is it the ultimate antidote to inertia? Why is it such a sure key to success?

The reason it is so powerful is very simple: an empowering promise cannot be broken. Never. Not once. Not even a little bit. Once made, it can't even be changed; the empowering promise has to be kept unconditionally. Its power comes from its absolute unbreakability.

To understand the power of this promise, you are going to follow the journey of seven ordinary people who came to me because their lives were headed nowhere in particular; they were all suffering from some degree of inertia. Their stories are based on real people, whose names, of course, have been changed. I have also had to doctor some of the facts of their lives to fit the message. I've had to play with chronology, juggle what they said, reshape events and even invent a few twists and turns, but I make no apologies for this. Unimportant details must play second fiddle to the message.

These wonderful people embarked, largely out of curiosity, on a course in which they hoped to learn how to make money. What they experienced was not a series of lectures on investment strategies or entrepreneurial skills but a gradual, self-paced realisation of the power of their own word. For some, this meant they could start to achieve their financial goals; for others it led in other directions.

Their first lesson was that getting rich is a choice. It is not a nice thought, a castle in the air, a whim of the moment or a daydream. It's a choice as bland and uninspiring as deciding what you will have for breakfast.

So, dear reader, you won't be sailing to Byzantium in this book or dancing with the tooth fairies. You will be asked to stand in the Choice Gap and make an either-or decision: either you will get rich or you won't.

You will also be asked to take as your companion on this journey only the truth — the whole truth about your life. It is this truth, as you will hear repeatedly in this book, which will set you free from your inertia and prepare you to make the empowering promise.

A final word on what I mean by 'getting rich'.

I do not own a yacht, a fleet of cars, or a villa on the isle of Capri. Nor do I have millions in the bank. But I have enough financial independence to be able to choose how I spend my life. In my mind, that makes me rich. My needs are met, and I always have at least one more dollar than I want. What would be the point of going after more money? You might argue that this would give me a greater number of choices. My answer would be that it is not the number of choices I have that makes me rich; it's the quality of those choices.

Only fools believe that money, in and of itself, will make them happy. Bigger fools, however, believe that they can live happily without it. That may have been true in the days of St Peter the Hermit, but in 2006, it's just not possible to fulfil your responsibilities to yourself and your dependants without money.

I believe that personal happiness is a product of the choices one makes in life. Money is, and always has been, simply a means of being able to make those choices.

1. the red pill or the blue one?

Start with what you have.

As a child I used to go with my father to the local council dump. I still have vivid memories of the old man who lived in a makeshift tin shed at the entrance to the dump. He spent his days doggedly scavenging through mountains of garbage. Although I was too young to know it, he was running a profitable little business. He was also the main reason I'd beg Dad to let me go with him — while my old man was busy emptying the trailer, the real old man would treat me to a VIP tour of the business. On each visit he'd take me into his shed and boast about his treasure, proudly holding up a crippled chair, a battered toaster or a limp picture frame, and telling me how he would fix them, what price he could get for them, what fools people were for throwing them away. To grown-ups he was a weirdo, of course, but to me, a six-year-old boy on Treasure Island, he was a land pirate, swashbuckling his way to a buried fortune.

An extraordinary journey can begin in an ordinary way.

One day I asked him if he had a real job, like my dad. 'This is my job,' he said. 'I make a living out of what people

6

throw away. Mind you, not out of what they throw away deliberately, but out of what they throw away by mistake. People just don't appreciate what they have.'

It was the earliest, and one of the finest, bits of wisdom I can remember. Translated, it means three things to me. First, you can make money out of anything. Second, to make money you start with what you have. Third, there's a treasure trove of valuable insights and moneymaking ideas waiting to be discovered in the most mundane, the most ordinary events of life, provided we're prepared to do a bit of 'scavenging'.

So it came as no surprise to me that finding a parking space in an ordinary street in a more than ordinary suburb of Sydney turned out to be the start of an extraordinary journey for me.

It's not the setting I would have chosen, because I can't think of anything I hate more than driving in the city on a Saturday morning, looking for a parking spot. And the very thought of shopping sends my blood pressure sky-high — minimarkets, supermarkets, megamarkets, gigamarkets ... to me they're all just different names for the same hell.

But there it was: a parking space.

I slammed on the brakes, turned in, and *then* hit the indicator. It must have been in that order, because I remember a chorus of impatient horns. Not that I cared much. Finding a parking space within hiking distance of my destination in central Sydney on a Saturday morning was such a moment of irrepressible joy that rational driving behaviour would have been the last thing on my mind. In any case, they were probably just jealous.

> If you put your faith in luck, you'll probably end up with neither.

'Right near an ATM! You little ripper!' I squealed, like an excited teenager. Clearly, I was having a lottery moment. 'Get out of the car, Toney,' I mumbled to myself. 'Get out before you find it's all just some nasty trick of the summer sun.' I leapt onto the pavement so gracelessly that I nearly twisted my ankle. It wouldn't have mattered if I had. The taste of victory was too delicious to be soured. I had come, seen and conquered, and nothing would spoil that.

But something did spoil it. What happened next always happens: someone beat me to the cash dispenser. Damn it. I should have known. It can be four o'clock on Sunday morning and someone will appear from nowhere and step in front of me. On this particular morning I wasn't going to bitch about it, of course. I had already been served a generous portion of luck and there was no need to be greedy.

They were an odd-looking couple, from behind: a slim woman and a giant of a man. One in tight-fitting elegant jeans, the other in billowing, brown, baggy corduroys. I watched from behind as the woman inserted her card and keyed in her number, while the man, who must have been nearly seven foot tall, practically had to lower himself onto his knees to read the screen.

> *If you're fed up with having insufficient funds, you're on your way.*

'Insufficient funds! I can't believe it!' the woman gasped, in a distinctly English accent. She turned and looked up at the man angrily.

He heaved his mammoth shoulders, nervously checked around for witnesses, turned to her and said, 'Ssh! Don't embarrass me.'

Enter an elderly woman, complete with lavender blouse, pleated skirt, matching handbag. Undaunted by the prospect of a three-person queue, Lady Lavender marched between us. Her eyes glowered, and I'm sure I heard her tongue click. Clearly, she had heard every word and she had every intention of letting us know she had heard. The couple ignored her, but I felt for them, because it was obvious that Lady Lavender was soon to make a public announcement on the state of their private affairs, probably over lamingtons at the local Ladies Auxiliary.

'Embarrass you? How do you think I feel? Insufficient funds. It's been the story of our lives. I'm sick of it, Mitch. Absolutely sick of it!'

I didn't want to hear this. They were embarrassed, and I was mortified. I was witnessing what to me was a near-death experience — having nothing in the bank. Trying hard not to be present, I feigned interest elsewhere. I am, by all accounts, a lousy actor, so it was no wonder Mitch snared me easily.

'Sorry, mate. She's always bitching about not being rich.' His compulsion to explain was almost pathetic. I felt like climbing up a ladder, putting my arm around the gentle brute and giving him one of those hugs that would say something between 'It's OK, mate' and 'Never mind, Daddy understands'. I reacted much more conventionally, of course: I just smiled. Or more correctly, the muscles in my face went into a benign rictus.

The woman, on the other hand, was chomping. She turned on him. 'Me? Bitching about having no money? What about you? It's all I ever hear.'

No matter how many times I rerun this scene, my mouth still twitches at what happened next. There I was — five foot seven, looking patently goofy, staring up at someone who could easily have abbreviated my five foot seven to something much smaller. But instead of evaporating, which would have been both polite and sensible, what did I do?

Without knowing why, I reached into my shirt pocket and offered them my business card. As Mitch took it, a sales pitch came from nowhere, jumped the gates and took off.

'I can help you if you're having trouble managing your money.' Oops. A riderless remark. I knew I was in trouble.

> Who says you can't remake reality? Politicians do it all the time.

My stomach somersaulted. It was a stupid thing to do. It was invasive, inappropriate and vulgar. It's what an ambulance chaser does. I wanted to sink into the pavement and dissolve away. Meanwhile, inside my head, a big ugly genie was rollicking with laughter. *What did you go and say that for? You might be good at helping people who already have some money to manage their lives better, but these people have no money at all. What can you say to them? They're hopeless. They're in a rabbit hole. Forget it. You CAN'T REMAKE REALITY!*

But politicians do it all the time, I remembered answering myself, quick as a snakebite. Not that I had much time to enjoy my witty little retort, because the war drums started. The woman snatched the card from Mitch, turned to me and breathed fire.

> If you only mind your own business, few will mind yours.

'So, you're a lifestyle coach? Well, thank you very much. For one thing, our lives are just fine, and for another, mind your own business. You odious little man.' I was in shock at my own behaviour, so I don't remember exactly what she said. In fact, I am not even sure she said anything; it was much more like a hiss.

I remember closing my eyes, lowering my head, expecting Big Mitch to pick me up with one hand and see how well I worked as a key card. Instead, he trundled off behind the woman, who by now had disappeared in a blaze of indignation.

I needed to sit down and take in what I had done. None of this was like me. I am not in the habit of making a fool of myself, and she was right. I had acted like a perfectly odious little man.

'It's over,' I said to myself. 'It's no big deal. Get a grip on yourself. Relax.' I took a few deep breaths then headed to the only café in sight, plonking myself down at an outside table, feeling as if I had just narrowly survived a pub brawl.

I had barely caught my breath when a girl in her twenties, howling toddler in tow, turned up at my table to ask for a 'spare two dollars'. *Not now*, I thought. *Just go away. I'm an odious little man. Can't you see?* I was definitely not in the mood to extend a helping hand to anyone else. But I'm also a big softy. I rummaged around my pocket, found some loose coins and handed them over, more to get rid of strident mother and screaming urchin than for any better reason. She snatched them up, tossed them quickly into her pocket, looking neither at them nor me. They could have been jellybeans for all the interest she showed. No 'Thank you', not even an audible grunt of gratitude. I was just a change machine to her. *Why the little* ... but I bit my tongue; I had learned my lesson. There was no way another riderless remark was going to be let loose.

> Why does life seem to smile on some and frown on others?

'You can't get away from them, you know.' A waitress had appeared at my table, order book in hand, shaking her head. 'They're hopeless. They come in here asking for handouts all the time. Waste of money. They'll probably drink or shoot up anything you give them anyway.'

'There but for the grace of God . . . ,' I started to say, thinking it was the perfect moment to preach a bit of compassion.

'Nothing to do with God. It's all in their heads,' she said. 'They sit around on their arses waiting for life to deliver a free lunch. Oh, they might get one, but there's bugger all on the plate. And it's never as full as the next bloke's. Then they spend the rest of their lives bitching about it, so they don't even enjoy the little they've got. Used to have a boyfriend like that. Bitched about everything. Hopeless.'

This was all too much. I just wanted to sit down in a sidewalk café, sip a strong, frothy cappuccino, read the local rag and put my now-shattered morning back together. But instead I got a dose of unsolicited street philosophy, spoken with all the elegance of a radio jock. Even so, I had to agree with her. On the evidence, what she said was probably beyond reasonable doubt; bitching breeds bitching. It certainly looked that way on that sunny Saturday morning. Everyone was bitching, and everyone else was bitching about everyone bitching. Even I had started to do it. My whole day had been poisoned, so I got up, paid and left.

> *Bitching catches on. Do it often enough and it latches on.*

I needed to walk it all off. Over the next few hours — and I don't remember how many kilometres of streets — I walked aimlessly, trying to come to grips with my thoughts. It was not long before a question had taken over my mind: All things being equal, why are some people poor and others rich? And if all things are not equal, which is probably much closer to the truth, then why do some people manage to rise above disadvantage and others don't? I'm supposed to know about personal development, but I had to admit that I really didn't have a clue.

We all know people who never have insufficient funds, and will never have to ask for a handout — unless, that is, some cataclysmic event turns them into desperados. Forget their waterside homes, yachts, skiing holidays and swanky private schools. Those things are just signs of their wealth. If they lose them, they get them back again. Wealth goes deeper than that.

> *And on the eighth day, God made the 'haves', the 'will-haves' and the 'have-nots'? Not likely.*

Money, plenty of it, is second nature to them. Why is this so? Why is there a special breed of human being that seems to be life's favourite? And another that is life's punching bag?

It occurred to me that maybe there's a whole day missing from the creation story: on the eighth day, perhaps mankind was divided into the 'have-nots', the 'will-haves' and the 'have-mores'. Some people are blessed with the Midas touch, others are doomed to plain old fingers, and the rest don't even know how to use their fingers. But why? Is life really so unfair?

Of course politics, economics and geography make life pretty unfair on a global stage. Of course there are all sorts of sociological reasons for the division between the 'haves', 'will-haves' and 'have-nots'. But surely life was not meant to be so unfair in a land of affluence, where there is more than enough to go around? I just don't believe it. I still suspect, as I always have, that this unfairness is *natural* — in the sense that it has to do with people's natures. People naturally assume roles that for some reason become permanent — the prey and the predator, the strong and the weak, the host and the parasite, the rich and the poor.

> Being a 'have-not', in a land of plenty, is a choice.

I must have walked for well over two hours, firing off random thoughts that crashed into each other like crazed billiard balls.

Everywhere I looked I saw possibility. A woman with the looks of a world-class model; a gardener pruning a hedge with incredible speed and dexterity; houses that could be done up and sold for three times the price; vacant and underdeveloped land; businesses just hobbling along when they could be expanding at the speed of thought; even lithe youngsters on skateboards performing like Olympians. The city was swimming in talent and possibility, yet only a few people would make the most of both.

I ended up in a suburb I didn't recognise. I was probably lost, but I didn't care, because my thoughts were pumping me with adrenalin. I took out my notebook. I always carry one, because if I don't hook thoughts when they come, they end up as 'the ones that got away'.

I have learned many methods of wealth creation, and I have taught many of them to others. Like most people in the personal development industry, I have studied models of achievement and excellence. Yet on that Saturday I couldn't, in one or two sentences — the so-called sales pitch in the elevator — describe the fundamental difference between those who have and those who haven't; between those who are going to make it and those who aren't. *If I could find that differentiating factor*, I thought, *I could find the way to move from one state to another. I could teach others to free themselves and move up the pecking order.*

> The fundamental difference between being rich and not being rich is more than just money.

Of course some people have sudden wealth thrust upon them. Aunt Josephine's pennies in the peanut butter jar turn out to be a fortune in rare coins, or you find a briefcase stuffed with a million dollars that just happened to be thrown into your garden without a forwarding address. At least someone in the world wins a lottery every hour or so. Yes, we've all heard those stories, and yes, they do happen. But let's be honest: only a fool lives in the expectation of this kind of thing happening.

> It's short-sightedness to dream only of a better hole than the one you're living in.

There are a lot of ways to grow rich: you can turn a simple business idea into a global brand name; you can take on a profession that is itself a big fat cash cow; you can take the money you have and hit upon the right investment strategy; you can go to a series of house auctions at the right time and walk away with the right buy. But these are just strategies, and they're open to all of us. There must be a basic piece of the picture missing, because many people who know how to get out of the poverty trap just don't do it. You can spell it out in capital letters, make them learn it by heart, draw up the plan, but they never get up enough courage to actually do anything. They can't bring themselves to peel off the label that has stuck to them all their lives. Even their dreams are limited — they just want a hole that's slightly better than the one they're living in.

When I finally got home that evening, with my notebook stuffed with ideas and a whopping parking fine, I should have been exhausted. Instead, I was exhilarated. I stayed up well into the early hours of the morning planning what I would do next. I was going to go after the Holy Grail of personal change. I was going to find out why life sucked for some and not for others. I knew it was a tall order — even presumptuous — but I was convinced I could find a truth that would make a difference to the lives of a lot of people.

My strategy was simple. Instead of focusing on the rich and the successful — there are libraries full of stories about them — I was going to discover why people who are slotted into a 'have-not', or even a 'will-have' position, stay there.

I started with the 'have-nots'. No one really talks about what makes them tick; their stories don't sell magazines or get-rich courses. But instinctively I felt that this was the starting point. I rang a friend who worked for the Department of Community Services. She suggested I go and live with people who were trapped by their own circumstances. So the following day I booked into what could most kindly be described as budget lodgings.

My room was clean enough, though not exactly out of *House and Garden*. The shared kitchen was infrequently cleaned, and always with the same rancid mop, so it was never actually clean. The air was thick with a gaseous concoction of cigarette smoke (even the No Smoking signs were covered in it) and rising damp. A television was ingeniously chained to a cabinet in what I presumed was called, somewhat inappropriately, the living room. The pay phone was missing the phone bit. The bathrooms were not exactly a benchmark in hygiene, but you generally came out cleaner than you went in. Such starless accommodation was to be my home for a week or two.

I could cope with all this, since I haven't lived a pampered life, but what I was not prepared for was the daily shock of people for whom life was a matter a survival.

I don't think anyone at Hotel Hopeless was aware of what I was doing. I pretended to be down on my luck, looking for work. Since most people there sat around all day, drinking, smoking and talking, I was able to get a wealth of information by just hanging around. At night, when things became a little rowdy — the police or ambulance occasionally turned up — I'd retire to my room and write up their life stories. After two weeks of this, the common theme leapt off the pages.

I will not trivialise the lives of complex human beings into a few sentences. People are multifaceted, and learning the truth about them is like looking through prisms — there are angles and colours and surprises everywhere. We all know this. I was not interested in why, as individuals, they were in the state they were in; I was interested in a far less complicated question — why, as a group, did they stay there? What had robbed the 'have-nots' of the power to change?

It was pretty clear to me what had trapped them. They were living in scripts they had written, dramas that never changed. They knew them word-perfect. These were the stories that gave their lives meaning; they could identify the

> The more you stick to your story, the more your story sticks to you.

beginning, the middle and the end. They were actors, forever playing the same part in the same story. It was all they knew. Change was unthinkable, so the script inevitably became, for them, an unalterable, incontestable, eternal, truth — that their lives sucked. They were on a mission to deliver this truth to the rest of the world. The more they bitched about their lives, the truer their scripts became and the more their lives sucked.

Sadly, however, they had built their stories on a stack of lies. They all lied. Go and spend a few weeks among social outcasts and you'll quickly learn that there is little or no honour among thieves. My fellow house guests lied about how much they drank or injected, how much they gambled,

> Your life is non-fiction. Bring in a bit of fiction and it's no longer your real story.

why they couldn't get a job, why they slept on the streets. They lied to their welfare case managers. They lied to me. They lied to their children. They even lied about how much sugar they borrowed from each other. They lied so much they were no longer even aware of lying.

Why all these lies? My theory is that they lie to keep their stories going. Lies are a matter of survival — not in the real world, but in the scripted dramas they stick to. They are addicted to their own dramas. With the truth, they would lose their stories and their familiar world of blame and excuses, and that would be unbearable.

Their biggest lie, their most powerful addiction — and the one they all shared — was that someone else had written the story of their lives.

So what did Hotel Hopeless teach me? It taught me to look for the lies that ordinary, 'decent' people tell about their finances to keep their own stories going. It didn't take me long to realise that those lies are legion.

My mission had begun: I would help people uncover the lies they tell themselves.

The inmates at Hotel Hopeless had a lesson for all of us about the circular logic of the stories we invent for ourselves. They were 'have-nots' because they had no power to change the script. They couldn't change the script because they had no choice. They had no choice because they had no money. They had no money because they were living in scripted poverty.

When I left them I reflected on the power of story in my own life. Despite my world of personal and business success, I too was locked into my own scripts. I had a script for my profession, for my family, for my relationships, for the meaning of my life. Like my friends back in Hotel Hopeless, I had assumed, so often, for reasons of comfort and contentment, that those scripts were true, indelible. The key difference was that I didn't bitch about my life. I didn't blame someone else for writing my life. I knew I was the author of my own script. This in turn meant that I had the power to rewrite it. I had the power to change the script, to choose a different storyline.

> When you admit that you are the author of your own script, you will realise that you have the power to change it.

So it was all about choice. This was the real meaning of wealth: the 'have-nots' do not exercise their power of choice, the 'will-haves' are waiting to exercise it at some time in the future, and the 'have-mores' wield their power of choice as a way of life.

The next people targeted for research were the 'will-haves'. I soon discovered that they are also in a prison of their own making, but one that is a lot more comfortable than that of the 'have-nots'. Theirs is a world I am very familiar with. The 'will-haves' have their working lives running smoothly, their finances sorted, their superannuation fermenting nicely, their children smiling, their gardens growing. But they are not rich, not yet. Their power of choice is all in the future, when either their chickens come home to roost or their nest egg is ready for hatching.

> If you can't choose the quality of your life now, you're probably a 'will-have'.

Their present world is not one of abundance; it is a world of sufficiency. Of course it's not a bad place to be: it's reasonably secure, it's sensible, it's pragmatic, and it brings a certain contentment. However, these 'will-haves' are just as addicted to their own story as the 'have-nots'. A lot of them also lied, simply by pretending that they didn't want to have more.

> Our world is one of abundance, not sufficiency.

I didn't have to do much work to find this out. A friend of mine who runs a newsagency was able to nail it in two sentences. 'When it comes to playing Lotto,' he told me, 'the only difference between the "will-haves" and the "have-nots" is the amount they can spend. They all want to have more.'

We all want more. What is wrong with that? Why does 'wanting more' have to be described as greed or materialism?

I talked about this to many people who were financially comfortable. Very few didn't dream of millions, and those who said they didn't were probably not telling the truth. It didn't matter how good their lives seemed to be; everyone bitched. These people bitched about the bills they had to pay, school fees, land tax, income tax, council rates — even though they could afford all these things.

> Face up to the 'want more' within you. It's not greed; it's fuel for a life of challenge.

It puzzled me, however, that they wouldn't openly admit to wanting more.

I discussed my findings with my colleagues, my mentors, my partner — anyone whose opinions I respected. They all had good ideas, but none of them could help me put it together in a simple theory. I needed a system, or a metaphor, to explain the basic difference between the rich and the not so rich.

Not long after, I went to see the film *The Matrix*. I don't know why — I'm not a great science fiction fan.

Strip the film of its pyrotechnics and the story is simple enough. Artificial Intelligence (AI) is the dominant life force. It created a computer model of our present-day world (the Matrix), hardwired our brain and fed the model directly to us so it could use us as its source of energy. In other words, our reality was nothing more than whatever AI decided it was; it existed only in our minds, because AI had determined how we should feel and act. We were living in a dream, created by AI.

Somehow a small group of freed humans who lived in the other real world — the one AI didn't control — decided to take on the machines and free the rest of us. They found a man within the Matrix (Neo) who, after learning how to beat AI at its own game, began the task of restoring man to the position of master species on the planet.

At some point in the film, the penny dropped. Three months had passed since the episode at the ATM, and I had finally found my teaching metaphor.

All this time I had been dealing with two distinct realities, two matrices: one for the rich and one for the not rich; one for those who had the power of choice and the other for those who believed they didn't. The basic difference was that the rich were in control in their matrix, while the

> Someone else writes the 'have-not' stories; the 'have-mores' write their own.

others were enslaved, artificially, in their matrix. To put it another way, the 'have-nots' and the 'will-haves' believed the story they were told or they told themselves, but the 'have-mores' chose a better story, a story that liberated them.

It was a fundamental choice of reality. There are two matrices: the Bitch Matrix and the Rich Matrix. The rich control the Rich Matrix and the Bitch Matrix controls the poor.

You aren't born into freedom; at some stage you have to choose it.

Morpheus put it this way when he said to Neo, 'You are a slave, Neo. Like everyone else, you were born into bondage, born into a prison that you cannot smell or taste or touch. A prison for your mind'.

That night I dreamed I was inside an ATM machine. I was trying to explain to others inside the machine that they were prisoners of an artificial intelligence, but of course they wouldn't believe me. They weren't aware of being controlled by the machine, and they refused to believe that the money they were so desperately seeking was just another form of artificial intelligence. I told them repeatedly that they all had natural intelligence far superior to the artificial intelligence that had enslaved them. (That's what ATM stood for: *Attend The Matrix*.) Why not break free of the Matrix? Why not make money do the work for you, instead of the other way around?

Money is just artificial intelligence; your natural intelligence is far superior.

I woke to the sound of the phone ringing.

There's a word to describe why I had that embarrassing experience at the ATM, why I went to see *The Matrix*, why I had that dream and why the phone rang on that particular morning: synchronicity.

Synchronicity is meaningful coincidence. It happens when the brain is on a

When you focus on what matters, it's just a matter of time.

mission, focused on seeking out events relevant to that mission. We all experience synchronicity. You can be thinking about someone and suddenly they ring you or walk around the corner. Or a book falls open at exactly the right place. It's not that everything that happens suddenly has a reason; rather, it's that we have geared our brain towards seeing connections between events. Coincidences have meaning in this state because our minds give them meaning.

Evidently, a chain of synchronicity was in motion. Why else would a group of ordinary people, whose extraordinary learning journey you are about to follow, come into my life, with neither invitation nor explanation, at precisely the time it mattered?

2. Facts first

'Hello. My name is Margaret. You might not remember me, but you gave my husband your business card about three months ago, when we were squabbling near an ATM machine.'

'Yes, of course I remember. You're ...'

'The one bitching about not being rich. Yes, that's right. We both do that. Well, Mitch — that's my husband — and I ...'

By the time our scheduled appointment came around, three weeks later, as if in an extraordinary chain reaction, another five people had joined the first *Don't Bitch: Just Get Rich Workshop*. I am still puzzled about why it happened so quickly. I am not one for cosmic forces and the like, but there was no rational way to explain why seven people were in that room on the first night, when it was only meant to be a pilot course, using Margaret and Mitch as trial subjects.

Cathy had phoned me from my favourite café in Bondi. I had stupidly left behind the folder containing introductory notes for the workshop and, fortunately, my business card. She asked if she could join.

About an hour later, Cathy's friend Andy phoned. This call was followed by one from Andy's boss, who had the unlikely name of Napoleon. Mercifully, I was allowed to call him Leon.

I wish I had met the sixth member of our group, Grace, in different circumstances: she ran into the back of my car — while I was in it. We chatted for well over two hours on the roadside, about everything except my broken tail-lights.

The seventh member, Phil, was a taxi driver. He had driven Grace to the first meeting since her car was still at the panelbeater, and was so intrigued by what she told him that he came in with her to the meeting and asked to stay.

In the workshop we were going to go straight to the facts of where we were in life, where we wanted to be and how we were going to get there. I wanted introductions to be as objective as a well-researched business plan. We were to present the facts about ourselves and ignore feelings. In this way, I hoped we would begin to replace our garbled, unstructured, discursive autobiographies with well-planned and objective biographies.

In other words, we were going to dump our stories and find the facts.

> On a bank statement, you are a number, not a person.

Looking at the facts of one's financial life, square in the face, is the first step towards getting rich; the complications of personality only confuse the issues. To put it bluntly, the forces of finance don't give a damn what your name is or what your dreams are.

I was cruel about it at that first meeting. I pinned a banner to the back wall of the room: 'On a bank statement, you are a number, not a person. Get over it.'

One way to realise how much power you have over your own life, I explained to them, was to get into the habit of talking about yourself as if you are on the outside looking in. The task of my enthusiastic seven was therefore to introduce themselves in the third person, using a name of their choice.

> Self-examination should be as objective as a good business plan.

The cardinal rule was that while we were together we were not permitted to use the words 'I' or 'we' when referring to ourselves; we had to use the third person — 'he' or 'she'.

I am regularly surprised by how effective this distancing technique is. People are actually much more honest about their financial lives when they talk *about* themselves and not *from* themselves. A release takes place that lets them study themselves rationally. After all, until you realise that money is just a set of figures on a bank statement — artificial intelligence, an objective, black-and-white set of numbers, existing quite independently of you — it is impossible to take control of money.

> Look at why you have no money from a distance. If you're too close, the facts will blur into feelings.

The technique creates a lot of humour while people are getting used to it, but in my experience it's the fastest way to move towards objectivity. We were not at this workshop to get to know each other, nor to share our thoughts or express our feelings. We were there to look at the facts of our lives, particularly our financial lives.

Grace went first. She was one of those students teachers love — a hurricane of enthusiasm.

'Hello, I would like to introduce you to Grace. She's twenty-six, single and a hairdresser. Unfortunately, Grace feels that her life is not going anywhere. There are no promotions on her horizon, nor any prospect of marriage. In fact, she's lost interest in her life. Her life looks like it's going to be the same for the next million years.'

> In the court of money review, nothing but the facts are admissible.

'Will the rest of you ignore everything Grace has said except the facts: that she's a hairdresser, she's twenty-six and single?' I said. 'The rest is story and exaggeration. Strike it from the record. We only want the facts. By the end of this course, you will all be such experts in the rules of evidence that you will be able to hang out your shingles and practise law.'

'Sorry,' Grace giggled.

The first task of the rest of the group was to cross-examine Grace and try to extract as much information as possible: she then had to write a complete dossier on herself in the third person. I gave them 10 minutes. The questions had to be rapid-fire, giving Grace very little time to colour her responses. The whole exercise was a search for facts, not for feelings or opinions.

'How much does she earn?'

'Does she earn overtime?'

'Does she pay rent, pay off a mortgage or own her own house?'

'What kind of car does she own?'

'How much does she spend on petrol?'

I was not surprised that Grace couldn't answer many of these questions. None of the rest of the group could answer the same questions about their lives either. All had very little idea about what was happening to their money — this meant that their dossiers had to be completed for homework.

> Money doesn't care how you feel. The state of your finances is cold arithmetic.

I am still amazed at the number of people who come to me after completing a dossier on themselves and talk about feeling calmer, having moments of insight, and sensing a greater distance from their money worries. My indifference to their feelings takes them by surprise.

'So what?' I say, pretending to be as cold as an Arctic winter. 'Who cares how you feel? For the purpose of these workshops your financial life is no more than a mathematical function. It either works to give the right results or it doesn't.' On a few occasions I have actually burst out laughing, but that is only because I am such a terrible actor. The point I'm making to them, however, is deadly serious.

By reducing their financial state of affairs to a collection of facts, was I over-simplifying things? I do not believe so. After all, the laws of physics are simple laws that govern our world: to every force there is an equal and opposite force; what goes up must come down, and so on. At the most basic level, human beings are obedient to very simple laws — just molecules doing what they're supposed to be doing. Even DNA is simple: it's a handful of proteins in different combinations. One's financial health is even simpler: money in and money out and the difference between the two.

> There are laws to making money, in the same way there are laws governing the physical universe.

It took about an hour and a half to get through everyone. Then we spent the rest of the evening watching *The Matrix*.

I concluded our first night together with some take-away thoughts.

'All of you are living in the Bitch Matrix. You are controlled by the artificial intelligence of money. Your task over the next few weeks is to conquer that intelligence with your superior natural intelligence; that is, to move into the Rich Matrix. Go home and think about this in relation to the film. It might not have been your cup of tea, but I assure you, once you get the point, it will end up being your bread and butter.' Either it was a very weak pun, or the film had already started to work on them, because no one so much as smiled.

> A behavioural matrix is a set of rules. Some become slaves to them; others become masters of them.

At the second meeting, my seven disciples were visibly excited. I used a small dinner bell (a bit like Pavlov and his dogs) to indicate that the third person rule was now in effect, and the second session began.

As long as you remain in the power of the wrong story you will be powerless.

My opening gambit, in which I explained the liberating power of facts, went something like this:

'The Bitch Matrix is a powerful narrative in which all of you are enslaved. You have subjected yourselves to that narrative, become part of its logic, and are moving towards its inexorable conclusion. The most fundamental aspect of this matrix is that it is a story; it's a powerful story, though, and the longer you remain a character within it, the longer you will be powerless, ineffective and unfulfilled.'

'A story brings with it emotions — highs and lows. The Bitch Matrix is full of stories and emotions. In the Rich Matrix, on the other hand, we are not interested in complicated plots and characters. We are primarily concerned with facts; they liberate us because they strip events of their drama queen dimensions.

'To understand this, consider your attitude to your personal expenditure. In the Bitch Matrix, the story of your personal expenditure has lots of possible turns — I need to spend money because I'm depressed, it was his fault, I simply can't do without that, etc. You blame overspending on your wife, the kids, life in general, even the dog. The excuses, the blame, the storylines are endless. In the end, you are bound to a story of your own making.

You can't control your personal expenditure unless you make it impersonal.
Think of yourself as an account number. You can feel good or bad about it later.

'But what if you just looked at the facts? What if you were to step outside the story and say to yourself, without any drama, or even any emotion, "This person — this Andy, this Cathy or this Phil, or, better still, this account number 0428765 — is exactly $127.47 in the red this month. What can this account number do to rectify it?"

'Don't put the answer in a story. Put it in a spreadsheet. Adopt the indifference of a number cruncher. Treat the figures and dollar signs as just what they are: numbers.

> Take the facts of your money story and put them in a spreadsheet, not in a novel.

'In the Bitch Matrix you give these numbers a life that they don't really have. They are then capable of doing things to you; they have power over you. They disappoint you, make you angry, even paralyse you.

'When you look at numbers as dead facts, they have no power over you, because they don't touch your emotions. Margaret and Mitch have, for example, given money real power over their lives by infusing it with emotions. They worry about it; they fight about it; they suspect each other of selfishness and duplicity because of it. It is, they admit, wrecking their lives.

'Cathy says she is unhappy because she cannot get together enough money for a deposit on her new house. But who cares if she is unhappy? Do you think her loan officer will care? The fact is she doesn't have enough money for the deposit on her house. The rest is just a story; it might be a great reason to bitch, but it doesn't get Cathy that deposit.

'A good example of how we mix money facts and money emotions is in personal budgeting.

> A budget is no more than a process by which you control your spending. It's not a bogeyman; it's not out to get you.

'"Budget" is a word that is charged with emotion for most people, because it means restraint — curtailing spontaneity, controlling impulsiveness. It's the opposite of indulgence, so it's no fun. Well, that's the story. But what is a budget, really? It's a simple control process. If you clog it up with emotions, it can't do the job it's supposed to do. It ends up like a blocked drain; it just won't work.

'As anyone who has worked in business knows, every process is made up of series of steps, from input to output. To show you how objective you must become about your budget, we'll start with one of those steps: the latte factor.'

'The latte factor,' I explained, 'is an important consideration in any budget. If you added up all the café lattes, the chocolate bars, and the little lunchtime treats you have every month, you'd be shocked at the total. And do you know what? It wouldn't matter if they were cups of dirty water or bars of dirt; your budget doesn't care whether you enjoyed them or not. They are money moved from the credit to the debit side. That is the only thing that really matters.

Think only of the facts of your spending; feel nothing.

'Facts, everyone. Think of the facts of your spending.'

'Mitch,' I continued, 'tell me about Margaret's latte factor.'

'She lives in that damn café with her friends,' he said. He looked at me as if begging me to take sides. 'She eats lunch there at least three times a week.'

Oops, I thought. There was going to be a slanging match.

'That's not true,' Margaret answered. 'What about him and his friends? What about him and his "just one drink"? And all those stupid gadgets he buys that no one uses? And the money he wastes on *his* lunches?'

'But Mitch works hard. He has to eat. And what about the money Margaret spends on her clothes?'

I had to call a halt to this quickly.

'You see what's happening?' I said. 'You have certain facts about each other's spending, but instead of looking at them as numbers, you see them as a means of winning a competition about who can assign the most blame to whom. You are both in the Bitch Matrix. It's all blame and emotion.'

They exchanged two quick daggers and fell silent.

'Now where were we?' I asked. 'The latte factor. Anyone for coffee?'

I don't know what they put in coffee these days, but my brain went into overdrive and I began to tell them about my own dis-empowering story — in the third person, naturally.

'I think that before we go on, I will tell you about Toney in the Bitch Matrix. Like most reasonably successful entrepreneurs, he had a string of failures to his credit (or discredit). In the beginning he used to get mad, depressed, angry, cursing anything that walked and anything that didn't'.

> The 'Why me?' story is rarely supported by real evidence.

'"Why me?" he asked. "Why can't I be like that bloke next door who started off as a kitchen hand and now has one of the biggest catering franchises in the city?" Unlike him, Toney argued, Toney had fresh ideas that attracted investors. There was no reason why those ideas shouldn't succeed. So he wondered what he had done to deserve all this failure. After all, he knew all about how to start up a business and how to make it run well. He had even written a book on the stuff. His business plans were supposed to work.

'Gradually, he started to believe that he was somehow doomed to failure. He poisoned the pure facts with emotions. Imagine that! An intelligent person believing that he had been spooked! That there was some nasty power in the universe that had it in for him! Just how stupid, how far away from the facts, was that? To think that he was so important that in the billions of planets in the universe, God — or whoever — had decided to focus on him, at number 42 in a tiny street in a suburb of Sydney. An all-powerful, all-seeing deity was spending his time tripping up Toney.

'Armed with his story, Toney eventually started to expect failure. He had plopped himself right in the middle of his story and become its slave. Toney was in the Bitch Matrix. Down the rabbit hole with a bunch of beliefs for which there was absolutely no evidence.'

'But his plans had failed. That was true, wasn't it?' Leon asked.

> When faced with conflicting interpretations, choose the one that takes you forward.

'Yes. The evidence was that his plans had failed. But there was no evidence that he was doomed forever to fail; that was a belief, passing itself off as a truth.'

'But isn't the truth a matter of perception?' Margaret asked.

'No, belief is a matter of perception. The truth is the truth. There are people who still believe the earth is flat; they can believe what they want, but it's still round. Similarly, you can believe that you are going to be rich as much as you like. Such a belief works — as we will see later — as a motivator — but it is not true until you hold a bank statement in your hand.

'I must repeat it: the truth is the truth, and belief is

> The truth is the truth; belief is a matter of perception.

a matter of perception. There's a big difference. The truth is that you're all struggling. The truth is that you can't make ends meet. The truth is that you are all probably financially illiterate.

These are the truths that will set you free. Not your beliefs — no matter how positive they are.

> In the Bitch Matrix you blame something else for failure; in the Rich Matrix you take responsibility.

'Toney also confused the truth with his beliefs. He interpreted the facts in one particular way and then cemented them together with superglue emotions. After every failure, convinced of his own beliefs, he raised his fists to the heavens and used a variety of the English language that's probably a criminal offence. He was in the Bitch Matrix.'

'So how did he get out of it?'

'He learned the difference between blame and responsibility. Blame has to do with emotions, beliefs and stories. Responsibility concerns itself only with the facts.'

I turned to the whiteboard and wrote:

> IN THE BITCH MATRIX YOU BLAME SOMEONE
> OR SOMETHING. IN THE RICH MATRIX YOU
> TAKE RESPONSIBILITY.

'You see, Toney's belief was that he was doomed to fail. Someone or something had to be blamed for that. Someone or something had to be the object of an outpouring of emotion. The truth, however, was much simpler: Toney had failed a number of times. Why pollute these facts with self-recrimination?

'It was useless to blame himself for what was happening, and it was just cowardice to blame outside factors. Instead, he took responsibility for all the facts: his so-called failure, his choices, his beliefs, his bank account, his café lattes, his messy personal life, his stress levels. He stopped blaming these things — treating them as magnets for emotion — and took responsibility for the cold hard facts of what had happened.

'Blame is useless. It is based on beliefs — your own highly charged beliefs — and it takes you nowhere. It's untidy, often vague and slippery, and therefore difficult to deal with. Taking responsibility for what happens and for how you interpret what happens, on the other hand, is based on the truth. It's tidy, often clear and fixed, and therefore easier to deal with objectively. In a word, it's useful.'

> Blame is based on perception; responsibility is based on the truth.

'Margaret's always told Mitch that,' Margaret said.

'See, there Margaret goes again, blaming him. And he will blame her back. Soon their latte factor will be their divorce factor.

'Toney had to stop doing what you're doing. He had to promise himself that if after a few months, the investors came to him and said, "Your business sucks, you have lost all our money and are getting no more," he would simply say, "I'm responsible for it". He wasn't going to blame himself. He wasn't going to get angry. He would look for the facts about why the business sucked and accept responsibility for them. And what do you think happened when he started to think facts, not stories?'

'He could think more clearly,' Phil said.

'Exactly. And that's when things took a change for the better.'

> You are responsible for whether you're rich or poor.

It was time to turn the talk back to them. 'So just how much of your lives are you responsible for?'

'Well, we're not responsible for our genetic makeup. Or natural disasters, such as earthquakes,' Phil quickly answered.

'We're not responsible for the lives of others,' added Cathy.

'Great,' I said. 'You're right. Although you are responsible for some other lives to a certain extent — your children's, the life you share — basically you are your own responsibility. It's taken us a long time to understand this, but it seems that we are responsible for whether we end up rich or poor — all other things being equal. In some parts of the world you are born into economic disadvantage that is impossible to escape, but in the West, no matter how much disadvantage you are born into, there is always a way out. Our plans might get spoiled by a few cosmic events, or a market crash, or an unexpected health problem, but the fundamental truth remains: we are biologically, intellectually, and (for most of us) socially equipped to be in control of our own lives.'

'Phil is puzzled,' Phil said. 'Some people have it, and some don't. Some people are more intelligent than others, therefore they make better business people and therefore they make more money.'

> Growing rich is, intellectually, as simple as understanding the difference between fact and fiction.

'Would Phil like to present the class with the factual evidence supporting that statement? I think he would have trouble finding evidence that intelligence has anything to do with being rich. There are many people who have done amazing post-doctoral research but are still poor, and many rich people who can barely read. No, the path to financial freedom begins with understanding the difference between fact and fiction, blame and responsibility.'

I turned to the whiteboard again and wrote:

BLAME IS STORYTELLING; RESPONSIBILITY IS
FACT-FINDING.

Fact: There are opportunities to make money.
Story: These opportunities never come my way.

Among the great things that being born in the West gives us are freedom and the responsibility that that freedom brings. Because of all the wonderful choices we have, we now have an even greater responsibility for the quality of our lives. The situation is different for those born into a country where life is a matter of subsisting. But here, all of us have the same opportunities.

Fact: Some people are actually born rich.
Story: I'm not one of the lucky ones.

It is true that some people are born rich, but why turn that into a story about not being one of the lucky ones? We are all born with abundant personal resources and the free will to use them. We come out of that labour ward with a clean slate, and although our parents and our educators might write some pretty stupid things on it, we're ultimately responsible for what sticks.

Fact: We are the products of our own biochemistry.

Story: I can't help what I do; it's in my blood.

> Luck is only a perception. It is used in the 'Why me?' story.

People also love to blame their biochemistry for what they do and don't do. They say they can't help themselves. They can't, for example, control their spending. It's like a disease, they say. Yes, it is a disease. Uncontrolled spending is also an addiction — like all addictions, it gives you a shot of dopamine. So it is a disease and an addiction, and you're right: it's biochemical. Going on a spending spree picks you up, like coffee, or alcohol, or a cigarette. That's why we become addicted to them.

But so what? The fact that it might have something to

> Only certain diseases in the world are incurable; overspending is not one of them.

do with your personal chemistry doesn't mean you're not responsible for it. If you think about how you feel when you go on a shopping spree, you are blaming your biochemistry. If, on the other hand, you take your receipts at the end of the spree and add them up, you are taking responsibility for a set of hard, indisputable, unemotional facts and figures.

A friend of mine, who spent a few years on anti-depressants, had this printed on his T-shirt: 'Stuff the biochemistry. I've got things to do.' That's an attitude rooted in defiance; he was taking responsibility for himself despite the fact that there were all manner of weird things happening in his body that he didn't ask for.

Even if it were not true that we're responsible for our lives, even if it were completely a matter of chemistry, believing that we are responsible would be a very useful lie. Believing it is a way to empowerment;

not believing it is a ticket to helplessness. Yet again, it's a question of which Matrix you choose to live in.

Once more, I turned to the whiteboard and wrote:

BLAME IS EMOTIVE; RESPONSIBILITY IS
NEUTRAL.

Blame and responsibility both deal with origins and causes. Blame, however, is emotive, while responsibility is neutral. You can't deal with the consequences of your decisions if you blame circumstances or others, and especially if you blame yourself: blame adds a layer of emotion, a personal agenda that clouds the facts. It's just too messy to be of much use. Responsibility, on the other hand, simply says A is responsible for B. We can work with this.

> Blame is emotive; it adds nothing to the money equation. Responsibility is neutral; it brings clarity to the money equation.

This is the kind of objectivity we need to liberate ourselves from our own stories. There may be all sorts of reasons why we did something (blame), but in the end, we did it (responsibility). And that's what we need to deal with.

There is a huge difference between the liberating fact and the enslaving story. A caused B doesn't make an interesting story; it's pure fact. It doesn't make us feel very important. But A caused B because of this and that, and if A didn't have such and such, etc, makes good reading, because it's pure story and we can revel in it.

To illustrate what I mean, imagine if you wanted to know where the nearest bus stop is. The facts in the answer should only be a matter of distance. A bus stop is the nearest or it isn't. But what if I started adding some emotion to it; perhaps someone I don't like uses the nearest one so I wouldn't want to send you there, or

> Without the facts, you won't see the problem, and if you don't see the problem you won't find a solution.

perhaps I only know one bus stop in the whole city and I don't want to be embarrassed by my ignorance. My answer would now be a lot more interesting and could even be the start of a decent film script but it's not much use to you if you just want to get to the nearest bus stop.

Addictions, such as compulsive gambling, also illustrate the difference between facts and the fiction we invent, and responsibility and the blame we indulge in. Have you ever heard a gambler say, 'I put my entire salary in the slot. I pushed the buttons'? No. Gamblers say, 'It got hold of me. The machines are evil. I couldn't help myself. I was so depressed, and my life needs that sort of escape etc'… Excuses and blame galore. Until a gambler says, 'I put the money in the slot, I pressed the buttons and I lost it all', very little can be done to control the addiction. Without the facts, people won't see the problem, and until they do that, they won't find a solution.

The way out of the Bitch Matrix is to stop the stories, desist from blaming and look at pure, factual responsibility. Margaret and Mitch blamed their relative poverty on their habits, their lifestyle, their extravagances, their inability to make a budget, the pressure of their peers, each other, the cost of living, the fact that Margaret didn't work, the fact that Mitch wouldn't take sandwiches to work. It was story after story. The facts were much simpler: Margaret and Mitch spent more than they earned.

Another distinction between blame and responsibility is that blame makes you powerless, whereas responsibility empowers you. Blaming yourself just undermines your belief in yourself, whereas responsibility puts you back in position as prime cause. Blaming external factors for your lack of money is just another way of saying, 'It was beyond my power to do anything

> Blame makes you powerless; responsibility empowers you.

about it.' You may, of course, be right, and there may be all sorts of external reasons as to why you have no money. Margaret and Mitch could find about a hundred. But so what? Where does that get you? You're still in a state of powerlessness.

Blame, even if it's well placed, will do nothing for you; it's useless bitching.

On the other hand, if you accept responsibility, you can actually do something about things. Accepting responsibility implies no guilt; it only assigns the agent, or the cause.

> Blame is as useless as bitching.

You've also probably been told to 'stop blaming everyone else — blame yourself'. That's a completely twisted notion of life. You shouldn't blame anyone — especially yourself — because that's still looking at events in a 'whose fault is it' way.

There was a time in her life, Grace told us, when she spent like a madwoman. Then she looked at her bank account and got depressed about all the reasons (or rather stories) why she was in such a mess. All she needed to do was say, 'I spent it. This is how much there is now', and move on, but instead she wallowed around for a while, and the blame, the excuses, the soap opera, just bogged her down.

Stories make great reading, but in real life they're just weapons of mass *distraction*, ways of keeping you inside the Bitch Matrix.

It wasn't until the next session that I realised that bitching, blaming and storytelling had been doing much, much, more damage than just keeping my seven from getting ahead financially.

3. The choice gap

Mark Twain once said that we should get the facts right first — we can always distort them later. He was not only talking about the art of writing; he was also referring to the way we interpret our experiences. The third session would therefore be devoted to showing how our interpretation of the facts, based on how we feel, determines how we choose to act.

> You can't interpret the facts until you know what they are.

I wanted to show how, once we extract the ground layer of facts from the many layers of filters we apply to those facts — our attitudes, beliefs, passions, values and dreams — we can recognise our governing story and get ready to move out of the Bitch Matrix and into the Rich Matrix.

It has been my experience that people are more ashamed of their mismanaged finances than of almost anything else they have done wrong in life. Friends, for example, will confide intimate secrets to you, if they trust you, but will rarely tell you their net worth. Try it. Ask your best friend what their net cash position is and observe the reaction. As you will read, it was easier to get my seven to drag long-hidden skeletons out of the closet than to talk honestly about the state of their finances.

Why do people treat lack of money as a shameful sin? Why is it so heinous that few of us want to talk honestly about it?

I suspect that people are reluctant to talk about the state of their finances because they know they're more likely to be dishonest about it than about other things. If they were totally honest with themselves about their credit card debt, about money frittered away on useless things, their mythical budgets and harebrained, money-losing ventures, they would probably not be in a financial mess in the first place. It seems that we feel compelled to keep up the appearance of a well-managed financial life almost as much as we feel compelled to keep up the appearance of our basic sanity. Until we get over the fallacy that lack of money is something to be ashamed of — that we have to lie about it in order to save face — we'll never have enough clarity of thought to rectify the situation.

This session showed me just how right my suspicions were. I rang my bell to announce that the third person rule was now operative and asked if there was anyone who would like to talk about an experience that had had a negative effect on their life. Looking back on it now, I did the right thing by not restricting it to the money world, because our money experiences are often much darker, more destructive secrets than we realise.

There was silence.

'OK, then,' I said. 'What's the best story in the world? What sells best?'

'Sex,' Andy said, and the class erupted.

'OK. I would like Andy to imagine that he was once unfaithful to his wife and that he has kept this hidden from her for several years.'

Andy rose to his feet, accompanied by hoots of disapproval.

Vague language keeps you outside the facts. When you are outside the facts, you are easy prey to your emotions.

'Ten years ago Andy cheated on his wife. She still doesn't know, and he has been living with this guilt ever since. It has been like a noose around his neck,' he said, as if he were delivering a bombshell.

'Cheated? What does that mean?' I said.

'You know.'

'Sorry. I don't. Did Andy cheat at cards? Did he steal from her? Did he have sex with another woman? What do you mean? Don't smother the truth with vague language — you'll end up asphyxiating it.'

'He had sex with another woman.'

'What does Andy mean by that? You're still too vague.'

'He made love to another woman.'

'Now, either he made love to another woman, or he had sex, or he did both. Which was it?'

'He had sex.'

'What is that?'

'He penetrated her?'

'Penetrated? There's a nice clinical word,' I said, somewhat sarcastically, pushing further down to the facts.

'He put his penis into her vagina.'

'Voila! So ten years ago Andy put his penis into the vagina of a woman who was not his wife. Is that what he did?'

'Yes,' he said with a slight giggle.

You can't say something is right or wrong until you know what that something is.

'So instead of the vague claim that he cheated on his wife, we know now that Andy inserted his penis into a woman who was not his wife.'

'Yes. But that's cheating. It's wrong.'

'Wait a minute. At the moment all we know is that the act of penetration occurred. Right or wrong comes after we extract the facts, which at the moment sound pretty bland to me. Organ A in Cavity B. Millions of people do that every minute. Did Andy know this woman?'

'No. He did not.'

'Did he meet her again?'

'No.'

'So it amounted to the rubbing together of two pieces of flesh, of people who did not know each other?'

'Yes.'

'Are there any other facts Andy should tell us?'

'Both Andy and the woman were drunk at the time.'

The class erupted again. 'Coward! Excuses! Chicken!' came from all directions.

'Is Andy suggesting that he was not responsible for his actions?'

There was a pause.

'It was his penis, wasn't it?

Another class disturbance; they were obviously enjoying this exercise.

'Yes, of course.'

'No one else inserted it but Andy?'

'OK. Andy was responsible for his actions.'

'So far, these are the facts. Ten years ago Andy inserted his penis into another woman's vagina, while drunk. This was a | Layer One: Beliefs | woman he did not know and whom he has never seen again. He accepts total responsibility for what happened.'

'Yes,' he said.

'Not a great page-turner, is it? Now we will see how he has interpreted this experience. First, what does Andy believe about marriage?'

'That it is forever. That it is about two people loving each other.'

'That's a word with a million meanings. Can you be more exact?'

'It means that two people make vows to be faithful to each other. This sort of love is exclusive.'

'Good. Now you are adding a layer of beliefs. This is an interpretation you are adding to the facts. What does he believe about his wife in relation to this?'

'That she would end the marriage if she found out.'

'How does he know? Is he a mind reader? Has he asked her?'

'He just knows. Women are irrational and unforgiving.'

'So Andy's real belief is that all women are irrational and unforgiving?'

Grace, Cathy and Margaret booed in unison.

'So because all women are irrational and unforgiving, Andy believes that his wife would chuck it all in over a one-night stand that happened ten years ago? That their marriage could not survive?'

'He would lose her if he told her.'

Layer Two: Values

'That sounds like a pretty strong belief to me. With those two beliefs, I'm not surprised he doesn't tell her. Let's move up a layer. What is Andy's strongest personal value?'

'Honesty.' The word almost ricocheted throughout the room.

'I can see that it must be a strong value, otherwise Andy would not have had the courage to stand up and relate it all,' I said.

'Can Andy see that the fact of his not telling his wife — of deceiving her once and continuing to keep that from her — and his strongest personal value are completely misaligned.'

'Of course.'

Layer Three: Passions

'Let's try another layer. What's Andy greatest *passion* in life? Not in relation to marriage, but in relation to life? What makes him leap out of bed in the morning? What is the one thing that drives him above everything else?'

'Andy is passionate about being a father. He lives for his two daughters.' Andy was playing his role extremely well, since in reality he was not married and had no children.

'Would it then be fair to say that the act of sex with a woman who was not his children's mother is inconsistent with his passion for fatherhood?'

'Absolutely.'

'Well, that was straightforward enough. Now, what makes Andy tick? What comes so naturally to him that when he does it he feels completely himself? What is his defining talent?'

> Layer Four: Essence

'Andy plays the guitar. He loses himself in it.'

'Did Andy feel this when he had sex with another woman?'

'Of course not.'

'Does Andy feel it when he has sex with his wife?'

'Yes. Their intimacy has inspired much of his music.' This was followed by a few mock violins.

'Finally, what is Andy's ultimate dream, the one to which he is willing to devote all his energies?'

> Layer Five: Dream

'To have his music published. And Andy knows what you are going to say. The few minutes of pleasure ten years ago didn't contribute to his dream.'

'You've got it. One final question. If Andy knew what he knows now about his belief system, his passions, his values, his defining talent and his personal dream, would he have chosen to have sex with a complete stranger and risk losing everything he held dear?'

'Of course not.'

'So why did he?'

'Because he didn't think about these things.'

'Exactly. He didn't pause long enough to make a choice. He probably didn't even know he had a choice. It was pure stimulus and response. Nothing in between.'

This session lasted almost three hours, and it was one of the most rewarding times of my life. One by one, I led each person through choices they had made in the past whose consequences were hanging over them. We searched for the facts — stripped down to the bare essentials — then added the layers of beliefs, values, passions, essence and dream.

Grace's story was typical. It was a full-blown drama to her, but a very dull version of a humdrum theme to the rest of us: Grace hadn't told her father about her boyfriend because he is not Jewish.

I challenged her to phone her father that night and tell him the truth. She resisted, cried, fought with me ... but finally agreed.

'The truth will set you free, Grace.'

(In fact, the truth not only freed her but completely surprised her. Her father said that he had always put her happiness above his own and he didn't see any reason not to continue doing that.)

The fact-finding theme became clear to them all: if they had considered their most important values before they had acted, the facts would have been different.

We were there, however, to talk about money, not to make public confessions. It was Leon who saved the class. He volunteered to talk honestly about his financial affairs. When he stood up and came to the front, he was noticeably nervous.

'Leon wants to talk about his money, doesn't he?' I asked

'Yes.'

'Why are you so nervous for Leon's sake? He's not even here, remember?'

'Because I am — sorry, he is — Andy's boss.'

'Andy has just confessed to putting his marriage on the rocks with an illicit romp with a stranger, and here is Leon, petrified to talk about money because an employee is listening!' This scored a good laugh.

'OK, then. Leon can't control his spending.'

'Too broad. Let's start at the beginning. How much does Leon earn?'

'About $85,000 a year.'

'Is he married?'

'Yes. He has two children.'

'Does he own his own house, or is he on the way to owing his own house?'

'No, he rents it.'

'How long has he been earning $85,000 a year?'

'About seven years.'

'And how much has he saved?'

Leon said nothing.

'Zero is only a number. Please tell Leon it has absolutely no power over him. So how much has he saved?'

'Nothing. Leon is in debt.'

'So they're the facts. We can do something with them. Does Leon keep receipts for what he spends, or track it in some way?'

'No.'

'Why not?'

'It's trivial. He couldn't be bothered.'

'Leon runs a budget at work, doesn't he?'

'Yes.'

'And he would keep a record of all outgoings, yes?'

'Of course.'

'So would it be fair to say that Leon believes he is accountable to his company for the money that passes through his hands, but not accountable to anyone for his own money?'

> Zero is only a number.

'Yes. My — I mean Leon's — money is his own. He can spend it any way he likes.'

'So Leon has a strong belief operating. He believes he is not accountable to anyone but himself for the way he spends his money.'

'Yes.'

'Up we go to the next layer. What is Leon's greatest passion in life?'

'Sailing. Leon spends a lot of time and money on sailing.'

'Can Leon see that his belief in his non-accountability is consistent with his passion for sailing? That there is no conflict here?'

'Yes.'

'Up again. What is Leon's strongest value in life? What drives his moral engine?'

Leon was intelligent enough to know exactly where I was going. He looked disturbed, as if the truth had suddenly slapped him in the face.

'The same as Andy: being a good father.' Leon was, in fact, a father of two.

'Is there a conflict between his belief in his non-accountability and his responsibility as a father? Is there a misalignment?'

'Yes.'

'If every time he went to lash out on new sailing gear he thought of what he could do for his two children with that money, would Leon still choose to spend the money on himself?'

He didn't say anything.

'Leon's belief that keeping track of his personal spending is not important is not consistent with his major value in life, and if we went on, I am sure we would find that it is also inconsistent with his sense of what he's about and the future he dreams of. The point is, he has a belief that throws everything else out of alignment. How it got there doesn't matter; what matters is that Leon is choosing to hold onto it.'

It was getting late and we should have been exhausted, but instead, we were all buzzing.

With a little effort, we can all start to bring choice back into our lives. We can stop making bitch choices and start making rich choices — choices that are aligned with all the layers we attach to the facts.

> You need to align choices about money with your beliefs, passions, values, essence and dreams.

Let's begin with a fact we so often forget: in the real world, we have a choice over every single moment. Think about that. Throughout the day, and perhaps our whole waking life, we have choices. In fact, life is largely a series of choices we don't even know we're making.

You, the reader, can make a choice right now. You can choose to stop reading and do something else. At work tomorrow, you can choose to march into the boss and tell him he has bad breath or burst into an opera aria in the work canteen. There's so much possibility available to you! Much of it is neither practical nor sensible, but it is nonetheless possible.

You not only have choice in relation to your actions; you also have choice in relation to your feelings. Most of us are so used to reacting automatically to things that we forget we can actually choose how we feel. You can choose to be happy, sad, fulfilled, frustrated, stimulated or bored. Try it. Next time you go to burst into tears in some crisis, force a smile instead. See how it changes things.

> You can also choose how you feel, how you interpret the world.

You make literally thousands of split second choices about your actions, feelings and interpretations every day. Apart from your body's automatic reflexes, everything you do is a result of choice. Of course you would lose the plot if you tried to keep track of all these choices, but if you're going to take control of your life, you'll need to start thinking about them. After all, these split-second choices are what make up your life.

Every act you choose to commit is controlled by how you feel. You choose to snap angrily at the cat because you feel annoyed. You choose to give your partner a kiss because you feel loving. You could have chosen to snap at your partner and kiss the cat! Which means you could have chosen to be annoyed with your partner and loving to your cat, but you didn't.

> What you choose to do is determined by how you choose to feel.

So why would you choose to feel one way and not another? Because you have chosen to attach a meaning to what is happening, to interpret it in a certain way. In the case of the partner and the cat, your partner curled up with you in front of the TV, and you saw it as affectionate. The cat curled up on the same sofa, and you saw it as annoying. You could have done it the other way around, but you didn't.

What you choose to do is a direct consequence of how you choose to feel, and how you choose to feel is a direct consequence of how you choose to interpret each event in your life. Choose a different interpretation or feeling and you'll take a different course of action. Clearly, with all these choices available to you, you have plenty of opportunity to take control of your life.

Everything about us is thus a product of the choices we make. We can control those choices or let them control us. They set up a chain reaction, so if we take control of one link of the chain, we'll control the outcome. If we don't, we're headed for helplessness.

> Take control of one link in the chain and you will control the outcome.

It would be both painful and unproductive to do this with everything in life. Taking control of some chains of reaction, however, can make a big difference.

Take compulsive spending, for example. If you learn to feel and interpret the moment of desire in a way that's different, it will lead to not spending money on a whim.

To be in control of a situation you must be in control of your choices. You choose the interpretation, you choose the feeling, and you choose the action. What was once a chain reaction will then become a chain of command. By intervening in chain reactions, you consciously exercise real personal power over your own life. Do this often enough and you move from conscious competence to unconscious competence, where having an abundance mentality, for example, comes naturally to you.

You are the person who has to decide whether you'll do something or not do it; whether you'll lead or follow; whether you'll try for the goal that's far away, or stay put.

It all starts and ends with choice. So let's get back into the habit of making choices. Here's a choice to start with: Do you really want to be rich? It's time to make a serious choice, instead of a half-baked wish. Take your time and think about it. But remember, your answer will depend on the meaning you attach to 'being rich', which will determine how you feel about it, which in turn will determine whether or not you will choose to make it happen.

> Do you really want to be rich?

You can go a step further and attach absolute importance to getting rich. It can become the focus of your life, until you have well and truly changed your Matrix. If you make it more important than anything else you do, you will give it a meaning that will guarantee a successful outcome.

It's up to you. What you do will depend on how you feel, and how you feel will depend on the meaning and significance you attach to the idea of 'financial freedom', or 'being rich'.

The consequences of embarking on a journey to financial freedom are unsettling. It's serious change. You can choose to interpret those consequences as liberating or oppressive.

The choice is yours: are you going to bring the meaning of financial freedom into your life, or are you going to think of this book as just another lot of personal development hoop-la? It is an either/or decision: do or don't. Beyond that choice there is just game playing.

And what happens if you choose not to be rich? What happens if you don't want to spend a lot of time and effort making money? Well, that's a valid choice and, for the majority of people, a wonderfully affirmative statement of their own authenticity. But it's still a choice.

If you want to be rich, then you must choose to be so. If you want to spend your life fishing or being a great mum or building things, then you must make a choice. In making a clear choice about what you really want, you will set a clear direction and destination, which of course will make the journey a lot easier.

So getting rich is only an example of the sort of life choice you can make. I have built this course around getting rich because it is the easiest human desire to turn into facts; do this and you make money, do that and you don't. Imagine the personal empowerment if you treated other life choices with the same sort of clarity that building wealth requires! You'd be unstoppable!

So getting rich is only an example of the fundamental choice we should make – a choice between a life fully lived and a life half lived, between the one you want and the one you don't. Make that choice, then let all your important choices take their lead from it and you're on your way to self-fulfilment, rich or otherwise.

Making financially sound decisions, or indeed any decisions that are important to you, requires deliberation; not talking to yourself, necessarily, but pausing long enough to make a deliberate choice between one action and another.

> Automatic behaviour is the enemy of financial freedom.

Recognising the Choice Gap between a stimulus and a response means pausing on the edge of a decision and suspending action for a split second. It means not doing something until you have assessed the consequences of your interpretation and your feeling: looking at the meaning you give an event, then at how you feel about it. You may not feel that you have an infinite number of choices when you're poised on the edge of the Choice Gap, but they're there. You just have to hit the pause button to see them.

Have you ever wondered how achievers manage to do what they set out to do? Their secret is so simple. In everything they do, they see choice: one thing leads to their goal, another

> Success comes by making choices during moments of suspended action.

doesn't. They pause, then choose the action that takes them closer to reaching their goal and reject the others. Freedom, and perhaps even greatness, lies in this Choice Gap. Achievers make themselves in these countless moments of suspended action.

If only we could manage the Choice Gap between stimulus and response. If we could just pause long enough to make different choices, we would really be masters of ourselves. I'm not suggesting

> Consider the power you would have if you managed the Choice Gap.

it's easy — we're all victims of chain reactions — but just imagine: if we could do this, how much power would we have? It's just a split second, but what an opportunity!

Do or don't in split seconds. It takes a split second to throw oneself under a train or off a cliff, or not. It's only a split second for the gambler to risk everything by doubling up, or not. It's a split second choice to break your diet, or not. It's a split second to undo six months of not smoking.

Consider a very mundane example. I know someone who took a week out of his life to focus entirely on breaking the habits that made him a complete slob.

He told me he cured himself by simply pausing every time he did anything that involved physical objects and said to himself, 'Everything has a place and shape. What is the shape and place of this thing?' That was the meaning he chose. Instead of giving these objects no importance, he chose to make them more important than anything else in his life at the time. So if it was a bed, its place being fairly fixed, its shape was to be made up in a certain way. If it was a letter from a creditor, it was to be filed in a certain place. The CDs on his desk had a home. The clothes thrown over the chair had a home. The linen had an optimal shape. It even went down to the look of his notes for his research, which were normally indecipherable and chaotic. For a whole week, at the expense of everything else, he focused on breaking the habit of this automatic behaviour. Nothing was more important to him. He figured it would be a week well spent. He continued his new behaviour into the second week, then into a month, and finally it became part of him. The only risk he took was the possibility of becoming anally retentive; it was a negligible risk he was willing to take. It was a small but significant lesson in self-mastery. He stood in the Choice Gap, facing choice head on, and chose meanings that helped him move forward, rather than ones that didn't. In other words, he controlled the chain of events.

Remember the film *Gladiator*? Recall the feelings of Maximus — played by Russell Crowe — in the Coliseum when Caesar mocked him. How it must have hurt to hear Caesar say, 'They tell me your son squealed like a girl when they nailed him to the cross, and your wife moaned like a whore when they ravaged her — again and again and again.' A

> Not even Caesar can take away your power to choose.

normal person, responding automatically, would have flared up in anger, doing exactly what Caesar wanted. But the Gladiator was in control. He stepped into the Choice Gap and chose when, where and how he would deal with Caesar. His response was on his terms.

It was the perfect chain of command of interpretation, feeling and then action. The Gladiator interpreted Caesar's words as those from a bitter and twisted little man, and gave it a meaning that put him, not Caesar, in command. The Gladiator's power came from the Choice Gap, the place of infinite choice and unlimited potential. He decided on his own course of action, a course of action that was less automatic and less out of his control. He chose to hit the pause button.

What self-mastery you would have if you could be like the Gladiator! Try it. Try it with the way you spend money. If you splurge without thinking, for instance, try timing how long it is between when you feel the urge and when you hand over your money. This is the Choice Gap. Then try widening the

> Widen the Choice Gap by turning automatic behaviour into timed events.

Choice Gap — at the moment there's probably not much time separating stimulus and response.

If it was 30 seconds the first time, aim for a minute the next time, then two, five, and so on. Keep widening the gap. When it's wide enough, you'll start to face all the choices about money that are available to you in those moments. Gradually you'll start to choose differently, because you will have learned the value of pausing long enough to make the choices that lead you towards greater financial freedom.

Each time you have to make a decision about money
— whether it's about buying a cup of coffee, paying a bill,

> Those who make
> money make
> choices.

going on a holiday or making an
investment — step into the Choice Gap.
Next, deliberately widen it, turning the
split seconds into minutes, then hours and
eventually days. Remember: those who make money make
decisions. Since they're in control in the Choice Gap, they
make the kind of decisions that won't unmake them.

Learning to choose again requires a lot of effort. With
determination, you will become aware of being at the
edge of thousands of Choice Gaps in your daily life. Soon
you'll be making choices consistent with your beliefs,
your values and your natural talents. Taking back this
power to choose is the beginning of making sure your life
is your own, built on your beliefs, values, passions,
essence and your life's dream. It's worth the practice. And
as you practise widening the gap, this little maxim might
help keep you focused: *I make the choices that make my
life and I make the choices that make me rich.*

4. The empowering promise

I was very nervous about our next meeting, because I was going to introduce the most powerful tool I knew that could kick-start a person along the road to greater wealth. It had taken me years of research and private practice to

> Where there's a 'will', there's also a 'won't'. It's between them that there's no way.

perfect this tool. I had tried it on a few of my clients, some of whom had taken it seriously and had, without exaggeration, radically changed their lives. Others thought I was mad. If by that they meant I was unbalanced, they are probably right.

I have learned that bringing about serious change in one's life is not a balancing act — that leads so easily to compromise. Personal change requires taking an extreme position: either you change or you don't. Either you do whatever it takes to change or you don't. It's a choice between *really* wanting to change and not *really* wanting to change. When you're on the edge of this Choice Gap, you must choose one position. There is no middle way.

> At 30, Bridget Jones is funny. At 70, she'd be tragic.

The homework I had set for my seven was to write down their own history of failure to change, including all the resolutions they had made, the broken promises, the aborted attempts at personal improvement, books read, courses attended, plans made. I called it the Bridget Jones exercise.

Cathy, who was quiet most of the time, which I thought was unusual considering she ran a café, revealed that she had kept a diary since she was nine. She was therefore the perfect Bridget Jones. She brought with her some five pages of short-lived successes and long-time failures.

After she had read a few of them, I interrupted. 'Thank heavens Cathy is so young. Imagine if she had done this exercise in her seventies. How would she feel?'

'She can't bear to think about it,' Cathy said.

'Why did she give up on all those plans?' I asked

'She doesn't know. There must have been a lot of reasons.'

'Actually, I think there is probably a single reason. Isn't it that her promises to herself have no power?'

She nodded.

'Margaret and Mitch are the same,' Mitch said. 'They've made a start at so many things, such as budget plans, ways to make money, even full business plans, but they never stick at them.' I waited for Margaret to make her usual response, accusing hubby of being at fault, but she didn't. *Ah*, I thought, *things are looking up.*

'This is another fundamental difference between the Rich Matrix and the one you're living in now,' I said. 'When someone in the Rich Matrix says they are going to do something, they do it. They don't fear the consequences, like paranoids, or wander around the outside of their decision

> Paranoids are scared to make a decision; peripheroids skirt the surface of their decision.

like ... — and I turned and wrote on the board a word I had invented — *PERIPHEROIDS*. They just do it.

'People in the Rich Matrix bring about change by acting on a decision to change. They say they will add another few grand to their nest eggs or launch their own business, or diversify their business, or go after a lucrative tender and they do it. Their word has power.'

'They're superhuman, you mean,' Grace said.

'No. Their power is in the promises they make themselves. When they promise to cut out unnecessary expenditure, they do it. When they set a savings target and promise themselves they will reach it, they get there. They are true to their word.'

'Then it's about self-discipline,' Margaret said.

'Right on. When they say they're going to do something that is consistent with their values, their nature and talents, they do it, because their self-discipline is rooted in their word. It's a self-discipline that is much more about saying yes than about saying no.

> The self-discipline that brings results is more about saying yes than about saying no.

'Remember last meeting, when I asked you all to tell me what you most wanted in life? You said things like love, financial freedom, health and security. All these are good, but there are even more basic things. I suggest that you might want to be true to yourself more than anything in the world. The rest will follow. It's a proven, strong foundation on which to build self-fulfilment.

'You see, you have the power to promise yourself to do anything sensible, with no backsliding, no ifs, no paranoia and no indecisiveness. So, for example, you will get the love you seek in life if you do not compromise. If you promise yourself that you are going to live a healthy life, and you keep that promise

> If you are true to your own word, you will get what you want: an unbreakable promise makes an unstoppable person.

by taking steps to achieve it, you will get the health you seek. It's the same with financial freedom. If you promise yourself — if you make an absolutely unbreakable promise to yourself — that nothing, absolutely nothing, can stop you, not only will you have taken one giant leap into self-empowerment, but you will probably become unstoppable.'

'So all we have to do is promise to be rich and it will happen?' Phil asked with not a little note of scepticism.

'In a way, yes, because that is where it starts. It starts with a solemn, unbreakable, lifelong promise that nothing can undermine. But it has to be solemn or it will be ineffectual. It's not something that you can play games with. There's no sunset clause in this contract with yourself. Either you will keep your promise to yourself or you won't; either you will do what you say you will do or you won't; either you will live in the Bitch Matrix or you won't.'

I wasn't sure how they were taking this. I was presenting them with an ultimatum. If they wanted to climb out of their rabbit holes into a whole new world, they would have to make more than a commitment; they would have to swear on their own lives, take an oath that would become the measure of their own worth, make an absolutely unbreakable promise to themselves that all the promises they would make — when made sensibly and thoughtfully — will be kept, come hell or high water.

> The great empowering promise is to keep promises.

'The first of all promises is to promise not to break promises to yourself.'

'OK. OK. We promise,' echoed from a few corners of the room.

'I don't believe you. First of all, we're not going to make such a big promise at this stage. You'll all just fall on your arses. The first thing we're going to do is look at what we mean by making an empowering promise, then make some small ones, which under no condition can be broken, and build up from there. By keeping little lifelong promises, you will see that there is real power in your word. Then you will be ready for the big one. The great Empowering Promise.'

'What's the Empowering Promise?' Phil asked.

'That you will keep the serious promises you make to yourself. All of them. At any cost.'

'That makes sense to me,' he replied.

'I guess it does,' Leon nodded.

'All of what we have said so far works together — control, authenticity, the Empowering Promise and your ultimate goal: permanent change. Once and for all to be out of the Bitch Matrix. Isn't that what you all want?'

'Yes,' they chorused.

'Experience has taught me that the happiness that comes from keeping vows, from being true to your word, is self-perpetuating; the more promises you make and keep, the more fulfilled you feel. It took me a long time to learn it, but I realised I was happiest when I said I was going to do something and I did it.

> The more promises you keep, the more fulfilled you are.

'Religion is built on the idea of unbreakable commitment. Think of the promises that monks and nuns made to God. If they vowed to travel to some foreign country to convert the heathens, they did it. If they vowed not to drink alcohol all their life, they refrained from it. They proved their worth to themselves, and to God, by being true to their word. Putting religion aside, wouldn't you love to have the same rewards of keeping solemn promises to yourself, of doing whatever it takes, with the same conviction and unwavering faith as if it were ordered by a deity, as if the meaning of your whole life depended on it? Wouldn't it be wonderful to achieve that sort of certainty in the power of your word?

'Religious people weren't the only ones who made solemn promises and kept them; not all solemn promises are religious. There was a time when we swore allegiance to absolute rulers, took oaths on our swords, signed our names in blood and entered inviolable fellowships. These formal oaths had real power, as action followed from one's word; those who swore did what they had sworn to do, sometimes at the cost of their lives. OK, maybe the vows they made were wrong, and maybe the consequences of their promises were sometimes horrific, but that's not relevant here. The point is that once upon a time, promises gave people exceptional power over themselves; their vows were, in fact, their power.

'You don't have to look far into the past to find the power of the promise. Think of the countless people, peasants and princes alike, who swore they would defend their country against invading powers and died doing so. And consider the number of marriages that have survived because both partners were true to their vows.

> The heroes of history gave their word and then took action. We all have what it takes to be a hero.

'So where has that power gone? Why don't we have it? Why don't we have the power to say we're going to change our lives and achieve the financial freedom we want? What's wrong with us? What has happened to that simple, 'Yes I will do it, whatever' that made the martyrs and the heroes of the past? Why can't we be absolutely true to ourselves the way they were? They discovered an inner force that gave them real power to take control of their lives and reach their promised lands. Why not us?

> 'The miracle, or the power, that elevates the few is to be found in their perseverance under the promptings of a brave, determined spirit.' Mark Twain

'If we could discover our ability to be true to our word, come what may, we would become truly unstoppable people.

'Actually, this power to be true to our word hasn't gone anywhere; it's just dormant. Everyone, including our little failing selves, has the power to do extraordinary things. That's not just psychobabble; it's a physiological fact.

'Consider, for example, what human beings do in moments of real crisis, when the so-called flight and fight hormones come into play. What power is at work that causes parents to leap into a swimming pool to save their children — even if they themselves can't swim? What is it in a man or woman that sends him or her into a burning building to save a child? And wouldn't most of us do whatever it takes to save our own mothers, even if the odds were horribly stacked against us?

'Aren't we all capable of extraordinary things?

'Think of your relationship with your mother. Someone attacks her. What are you going to do? Say, 'I don't have what it takes to be a hero. Sorry Mum'? No. You probably wouldn't think twice, because although you may occasionally forget it and you may never be asked to prove it, in such circumstances you're capable of unimaginable self-sacrifice.

'Luckily, most of us won't ever be put in a situation where our survival depends on accessing that power, so the chances are we'll spend life without really knowing our own strength. After starting so many change programs in my life, I'd have given anything to know some of that strength. Others had the power to change, to make radical, fundamental, lasting change in their lives, so why couldn't I? It seemed everyone else was blessed with willpower, and I had missed out. I sometimes wonder what I could have achieved in my life had I discovered much earlier that the power to achieve rests entirely on the power to be true to your word, especially in the promises you make to yourself.'

> If you don't use your own strength, you'll never know how strong you are.

'I'm intrigued to know how you reached this conclusion,' Margaret commented.

'I started with two basic assumptions: I had to change and I could change. The next step was to find out how to make it happen. I realised that those with religious purpose in a monastery, an ashram, yeshiva or madrasa actually do exactly what successful people do in their secular lives — they make a promise and live by it. They focus on their intention with passion, commit themselves to the supremacy of their own word and go out to do whatever it takes. The answer, therefore, was as radical as it was simple — I would go in search of the power of a special kind of promise — the one that brings about permanent change.'

Andy was next to speak. 'Toney, if you told us exactly what promises we had to make in order to grow rich, we'd keep them. We don't need to be saints.'

> The saintly and the successful have the same strategy: they commit themselves to their word and then keep it.

'I bet you wouldn't keep them. This program tackles change at a much deeper level. We will revisit those rules when we write our rulebooks together. But they are useless until you have discovered the power to keep them. Knowing what they are is easy — being able to keep them in order to bring about a permanent shift from the Bitch Matrix to Rich Matrix is a different story.

'So I can't help you unless you accept from the beginning that change, if it is real and permanent, has to occur at the deepest level of yourself. It is not like changing your clothes or changing your favourite cereal brand. If you think it is just like that, you will, without any doubt, achieve nothing.

> The surface of a person's life is littered with broken promises because that's where they were made.

'Psychiatrists (and Christians) have a name for a point in one's life when complete conversion takes place, when one's fundamental beliefs are changed and a new direction is taken. They call it *METANOIA*.' Another of my favourite words went up on the whiteboard.

'*Metanoia* is a powerful, life-changing experience; a point of departure from the old, discarded self. The conversion of St Paul on the Road to Damascus, from persecutor of Christianity to its evangelist, is the classic example of *metanoia*. If you want to move out of the Bitch Matrix, set your eyes on *metanoia*. Be warned, though. It's radical and it's disruptive, and getting rich isn't what it's about.

'The word *metanoia* means personal metamorphosis; it's about a transmutation, a transformation. You've already listed your attempts to break habits, and how they last for a while, but then you return to the habit, often with a vengeance. These relapses have a simple explanation: you've tried to change something which runs deep by applying a simple switch at the surface. No way.

'People who have been living on the breadline all their lives won't go much over that line if all they do is learn someone else's behavioural rules of wealth creation. To step over that line permanently, you have to work on the self, not just the behaviour. The rich aren't rich only because they do certain things; they're rich because they're fundamentally in tune with themselves in the context of abundance. They live in a Rich Matrix.'

> It's the self that changes the behaviour, not the other way round.

'But I don't want to change my life,' Margaret said. 'I just want to start making money.' I noticed that Margaret was more attentive than ever.

'First, you forgot to use the third person. That's OK. Second, change doesn't work like that. Bitching — which is nothing more than an addiction to a particular worldview — is so much part of you that giving it up will mean big changes in your life. Since you can't break its stranglehold — you've attempted that before — you have to change yourself.

> Bitching about life is like any other addiction: it enslaves you.

'People who break this addiction to their own sense of inadequacy through *metanoia* invariably experience this release from the Bitch Matrix stranglehold as something new and radical in their lives. Many ex-bitchers say they believe they can do anything once they're out of its grip. When you finally make the commitment, you're in for the same joy of self-efficacy. Something in the deepest recess of your core being, where an addiction has you enslaved, will have changed forever.

> Metanoia is an awakening, a rite of passage, a rebirth.

'*Metanoia* will bring new vision into your life. A decision to work towards such an experience, with its lifelong consequences, is therefore not to be made lightly.

'There are only six weeks to go before you make the Empowering Promise, formally and publicly avowing an unbreakable lifelong commitment to your own promises; to break any of these promises would mean admitting that you aren't worth your word. So, six weeks from now, on the last day of this course, you will begin a new life of action, because on that special day, in front of everyone — but more importantly in front of yourself — you will take a vow never to break a promise to yourself again.'

'That's crazy. What if we do break it? We'd feel like shit,' Leon said.

'Hold on. After you've made the Empowering Promise, if you think you are going to break a promise to yourself, you don't make that promise. It's much more important to keep the Empowering Promise, even if it means making very few promises for the rest of your life.

'If you aren't prepared to treat the Empowering Promise with this level of seriousness, you're wasting your time. Don't attempt to give up bitching, to leave the Bitch Matrix, unless you're utterly, utterly, serious about it. There's no exit clause once you make the kind of commitment being proposed here. Don't have in the back of your mind that you could forgive yourself if you break your serious promises. Absolving yourself and recovering your self-esteem, if you break a vow of this kind, will be much more difficult than keeping the promise in the first place.

'So there's a much deeper change we're going for here than just giving up your addiction to bitching about life. Keeping your word — for the rest of your life — is what matters. The test of real conversion, therefore, will come once you make the choice to be true to your promises — all of them.

> True conversion allows no reversion.

'Whether you want a million dollars, or to be a successful skier, or to be the best mum that ever walked this planet, it all starts with the most basic of all promises: the promise to yourself to keep the promises you make. To promise to keep the promises you make is the beginning of great personal power. The rest of your path to wherever you're going is just strategy.

'So will you stick to the ultimate promise to yourself or not? Will you, in another six weeks, be able to say to yourself that you're going to keep every single promise you make to yourself for the rest of your life? If you understand what *metanoia* is, you will realise how serious a step that will be, because the power of that promise lies in its absolute unbreakability.

> A metanoic promise is absolutely and unbreakably your own.

'If you're wise, you will only make promises you know you can keep. If you make all sorts of empty promises or treat your promises lightly, you will end up undermining your self-confidence and robbing your word of its power.

'To conquer your inertia and powerlessness, you must close off all possible avenues of retreat. Only then can you be sure to keep alive the metanoic spirit, which is essential to success.

> Breaking your word to yourself is being not true to yourself.

'Ahead of you is the joy of looking back over years of your life and saying, "I said I would do it and I did. I was true to myself. I was true to my word." The only way you will get that million, run that marathon, succeed in your career, is if you begin with the most fundamental promise — the promise to be true to yourself. Then, with that power behind you, you can make the other promises that will take you towards your goal.

'The metanoic path to self-mastery won't only bring you freedom from addiction to bitching; it'll also bring the indescribable, lasting joy of being reinstated as your own master. *Metanoia* is thus a complete change of matrix.

'Naturally, *metanoia*, being a radical change to belief and the behaviour caused by that belief, will hurt.

> Since radical change is rebirth, it will carry the pain of birth.

All measurable, decision-based change, from a simple behaviour modification to a complete reinvention of yourself, requires absolute commitment to new beliefs, which means full-on effort.

'The change can be gut-wrenching. You're not going to get a one-day "high" from this. It's not going to give you the kind of short-lived sparkle you get from motivational hype.

> Forget a one-night stand with your word. Think rather lifetime marriage to it.

'Think about what it's like to make a decision that radically alters a belief or an established lifestyle pattern, and that you're obliged, by your own choice, to follow to the grave. That's forever — a concept few of us have ever entertained in seriousness. If you focus on its meaning — everlastingly, always, eternally, perpetually, ceaselessly, without end — it will make you shudder. There's no divorce court, no termination of contract and no exit clause; you're committed to a lifestyle change, and that change is forever.

'Successful *metanoia* depends on such extreme commitment. It sounds weird, obsessive, even psychotic, some might argue. Of course it does, because it's the talk of the desperate. But if you're desperate to get out of the Bitch Matrix, really desperate, you're at the right stage to make this commitment.

> The truly successful and the truly desperate have one thing in common: they're capable of anything.

'Being desperate is actually an optimal state to be in — real change is most possible when you're through playing games. You go to the bank and there's nothing in it or you've come to a point in your life when you're absolutely fed up with failure. These are desperate moments in your life, when you're actually ready to do your utmost.

'So if you're not desperate now, try to imagine a time in the future when you will be, because if you don't have a sense of urgency, the wheel of failure might just keep on turning. Recall what Billy Graham said was the most surprising thing about life — its brevity. It doesn't matter if you're 10,

> The most surprising thing about life is its brevity.

20, 50, or 90 years old, you don't have time to waste on failing, so get desperate and start promise-keeping.

'Promise-keeping is about the joy of shaping, even reinventing, yourself and of taking responsibility for your own behaviour — indeed, for your whole life. Each time you reinforce your will over your life, not just by giving up bitching, but by getting out of any other ruts you might be caught in, you'll have a taste of that joy.

'When you begin to replace the pain of bitching with the joy of self-mastery you'll have found another ingredient of human happiness. It's a winner's joy; a deep and private confirmation of your own worth. In these moments, only you will be aware of the profound transformation taking place. They are *your* moments, because it's you achieving "greatness" in your own world; you're completely in charge, however momentarily, of your own life. It's a secret, recurring joy with which few others compare.

'Self-efficacy is the ultimate goal of *metanoia* and the Empowering Promise.'

There was a knock at the door.

'That must be our surprise guest,' I said, moving to the door to let her in.

'Everyone, this is Tamara. No time for introductions, so it's over to you, Tamara.'

> Self-efficacy is the fruit of promise-keeping.

Tamara is what is conventionally called a knockout. Not only is she beautiful and intelligent, she's also one of the most compassionate and compelling people I have ever met. A successful lawyer to boot, she is my number one testimonial to the truth of what I had been saying.

She took over the floor, and in less than a minute had everyone captivated.

Without skimping on honesty, she told us about her own discovery of the empowering promise.

She was not, clinically speaking, an alcoholic, she said, but she knew she hadn't had a day without a drink for over 15 years. She spent weeks thinking about what her life would be like if she just gave up drinking altogether. She had no practical or moral reason for doing it, since it didn't ostensibly affect her life, and she was far from a puritan. She simply no longer wanted to be a drinker; but she knew that being a non-drinker would radically alter her life. Her social life would be different, her moods would change and even her sleep patterns wouldn't be the same.

She spoke about the day she was in my office, on the point of tears, because she knew the day was coming when she would be giving up alcohol altogether. If you have understood the meaning of *metanoia* — a radical life-altering decision — you'll probably wince at the implications of what she was about to do. Imagine deciding never to drink alcohol again (a course of action not recommended for wine waiters or vignerons). One of your greatest social pleasures would be lost to you forever. No more delicious red wines quaffed in candlelight, no more cold beers with your friends. For most of us, such a decision wouldn't be appropriate, but for Tamara it was. It might not work for you (it certainly wouldn't for me), but for her it was the beginning of *metanoia* — the departure point from her old self.

She explained to us what such a serious decision would mean in her life. She tried it for a few days, then for a few weeks, and it hurt. It hurt, she said, because she hadn't yet taken on a zero-option mentality.

She planned a specific day when she would finally renounce one of her life's pleasures. She remembered me cautioning her against her extremist position of zero-option commitment, warning her it was 'over the top', but in her heart she knew her decision would bring her incredible self-respect.

She took the promise.

'I remember the day as clearly as the day I took my wedding vows.'

The joy of self-efficacy! There are few comparable emotions. Tamara told us how she had discovered a force inside herself that years of self-indulgence had stifled. She spoke about a new power to get things done, a pervasive self-confidence and an abiding optimism about the rest of her life. Best of all, her career took off and the money flowed.

It was therefore not about the drink, she said. Her decision was about self-mastery, and that was the beginning of her success.

In 20 minutes she had done more for my seven than I had done in four weeks.

I took over to close off the session.

'When you make a metanoic decision, in whatever area in your life you choose (not just wealth), you can expect to feel the same joy of self-efficacy that Tamara felt.

'This long session can be summarised in one sentence: Freedom from failure, from the broken promises you make to yourself, the half-baked ambitions you never realise and the goals you never reach, begins with the radical choice to become an absolute slave to your own word.'

5. No small change

Benjamin Franklin once said that self-improvement is about change, and in order to be perfect, one must change often. To achieve this ideal state (which, of course, we never will), we would have to go on changing until our last breath. This is probably just another way of saying that change is evidence of life, or as another wise observer of human nature, Aldous Huxley, put it, the only completely consistent people are dead.

> Permanent change involves planning, practising and perfecting new behaviour.

Real, permanent change doesn't involve a sudden bolt-of-lighting frog-into-prince bit of magic. It is slow and deliberate. It is bit by bit. The only sure way to change the big picture is pixel by pixel. In this sense, no real change is small; every little bit of change will change the whole picture.

If leaving the Bitch Matrix is to be permanent, the behavioural change must be planned, practised and perfected at its most basic level, one step at a time. Trying to walk before you crawl or trying to win the Tour de France before you graduate from a three-wheeler obviously won't work.

You would think that because coping with change is such an important life skill, we would have learned all about it at school; that it would have been taught to us as a fundamental survival strategy. After all, long after we've forgotten algebra, the sonnets of Shakespeare and the Periodic Table, our personal happiness will still depend very much on our ability to embrace all the changes that take place in our lifetime — biological, intellectual, technological and social. If life is a process of self-discovery, bringing with it endless opportunities to change and grow, it follows that self-fulfilment involves embracing the changes that self-discovery brings.

My task, therefore, was to equip my enthusiastic seven with a reliable road map for personal change. How does change work? What could they expect to experience? How could they kick-start the process?

There are many well-honed and recognised models for behavioural change. I presented them with a hybrid of what, in my opinion, has worked with a reasonable degree of consistency.

Both the Bitch Matrix and the Rich Matrix have their rules. These rules are behavioural. Do this and you're in the Bitch Matrix; do that and you're in the Rich Matrix. I challenged each of my students to identify and change just one small, unwanted behavioural pattern — something as simple as always putting their car keys in the same place.

But first, they had to listen to, and wait for, the self-instructing mind to deliver, in its own time, an ingrained unwanted habit that they needed to change.

Needless to say, everyone found one. Changing this behaviour, however, was much more than a class exercise. If there was one thing I wanted them to take away from this series of workshops it was that

> Change is either permanent or it's a waste of time.

change is either permanent or it's a waste of time. I said it so many times that I felt like a nagging parent. This was not a course about how to get rich in a month; it was about how to make a permanent change to one's self that would render it fit for a world of abundance.

Their target behaviour was to be changed forever, and they had to thoroughly understand the seriousness of that. They would have to take time to think about the implications of the change they were choosing, rehearse their new behaviour and build a vision of their changed selves.

I started the session by explaining what they were in for.

> Changing behaviour is a process of withdrawal, relearning and rehearsal.

'Rarely do people change their behaviour suddenly. Changing behaviour isn't like changing your clothes. Years of reinforcement have gone into forming most behaviour, and there's no simple on/off switch to reverse that history. Theoretically, you should be able to just step out of the Bitch Matrix and cross over to the other side. In practice, however, it doesn't work like that. You need to be thoroughly prepared for what's on the other side.

'Let's start by examining the nature of behavioural change. Basically, there are two ways to change: either you unlearn your present behaviour or you learn new behaviour to replace the old. The first method makes change comparable in difficulty to unlearning how to ride a bicycle. You may swear

> Habits are based on patterned behaviour deeply rooted in memory.

that you'll never pick up a bicycle again, and you may stick to that, but the memory of how to ride is indelible; it will be part of you forever. In fact, if you attempt to unlearn how to ride, the skill of riding will be reinforced in your memory even more strongly. Similarly, trying to unlearn an addiction, or years of inappropriate habit, is almost impossible, which is one reason why there are so many failures. As an addict to bitching about life, you've been doing it for years. You can't possibly "unlearn" it just by trying to forget your present attitude.

'The second method of change, learning new behaviour to replace the old, is much more effective. It's

| Real change is disruptive. |

fuelled by a surge of commitment and followed by a learning process. The model we'll use for learning how to bring about real change applies to all learning, from habit reform (such as learning to be a non-smoker), to developing new intellectual skills (such as learning a foreign language), life management skills (such as learning to manage your time) and a complete change of worldview (such as moving from the Bitch Matrix to the Rich Matrix).'

HOW TO CHANGE

1   Define the competence that you seek.
2   Define the new behaviour that expresses the competence you seek.
3   Pause in the Choice Gap and deliberately choose your new behaviour.
4   Begin practising your new conscious behaviour.

Eventually your new conscious behaviour will become new unconscious behaviour.

'All of you were supposed to identify a behaviour you would like to change. Any volunteers?'

Grace bounced up. She was always such a delight. Everything she did was accompanied by a gust of energy.

'Grace discovered that she has the habit of splurging the day after payday. She's been doing it for years. It suddenly dawned on her that it's been happening as regular as clockwork.'

'There's probably a significant belief about income lying under that behaviour, but we will put it aside for the moment. You have actually passed the first stage of change — the so-called *unconscious incompetence* stage — because you now know that you've been incompetent with your money; that is, your incompetence is no longer unconscious. You're in the second stage of change, called *conscious incompetence*. Up until today you weren't aware of doing this, but now you know, right?'

'Grace had no idea that it was a habit. She just did it.'

'Good. So does Grace want to change this habit?'

'You bet. She never splurges on anything useful. Usually stuff that makes her fat.'

'Can Grace suggest a replacement behaviour?'

'Nope.'

'Well, how about getting into the habit of paying her bills on the day that she normally splurges. Or how about splurging on the day immediately *before* her next payday, not after it.'

I turned to the others and asked, 'Does anyone know what this involves?'

Phil raised his hand. He was the most conservative of the group and always behaved like a dutiful student. I wondered about him; he seemed such a loner.

'Grace has to practise making a choice in the Choice Gap.'

'What would that involve, exactly, Phil?'

'She would have to pause before she spends her pay. She has to make a conscious decision to choose alternative behaviour.'

'And if she does choose to pay her bills first, she will have embarked on the *conscious competence* stage. She will be experiencing, I expect for the first time, her ability to spend her money competently.'

'How is Grace supposed to remember to do that?' Grace blurted out.

'Why did Grace remember to put her clothes on before she left the house?' I asked.

'She didn't have to remember. It's a habit. She's also not a pretty sight without them.'

'Did Grace always put clothes on automatically? If her mother hadn't dressed her when she was a toddler, wouldn't she have run starkers out into the garden?'

Grace giggled. 'Probably.'

'Her competence as a dresser was learned. She practised it until it became so natural that it was unconscious. With rehearsal and some parental guidance, she changed from a bare-bottom wild two-year-old to a respectably clothed human being. Eventually, she moved into the *unconscious competence* stage where putting clothes on before she went out in public was automatic.

'Consumer behaviour works in exactly the same way. You become aware of a need — or a want — you didn't know you had, then you go out and buy the product that fulfils this need. You use it and learn its benefits. Gradually, it becomes part of your life.

> When the pain of not changing is greater than the pain of changing, it's time to change.

'Getting out of the *unconscious incompetence* stage — knowing you need to learn new behaviour — is the beginning of the change experience. You realise it's time to change your behaviour when you start to entertain the idea of new behaviour or admit that something is wrong.'

Phil raised his hand again. I wished he wouldn't do that.

'How do you know when you're ready to change?'

'There's a litmus test. If your present behaviour is causing you much more unhappiness than the effort or discomfort required by any change protocol, you're ready to change. In other words, when the pain of not changing is greater than the effort to change, you're on the brink of a change decision. If the pain of continuing to be without money — or, more poignantly, continuing to let yourself down — is greater than the pain of a few weeks or months of conscious effort and self-denial, you're ready to change.'

Mitch was looking bored, unconvinced.

'Would Mitch like to say something?' I asked.

'Yeah. Mitch doesn't see how this is going to make him rich.'

'If the pain of not being financially independent is strong enough, it will be a real stimulus to becoming financially independent,' I answered. 'But let's not play with theories; let's experience it.'

It was time for a bit of theatre. I asked the class to stand up and find a place in the room where they would feel most comfortable and most private. They had to remain standing. My music was ready to roll, and so, with a few breathing exercises, I launched them straight into a state of simple relaxation. It was time to let their imagination reinforce my teaching.

I told them to put aside the small thing they wanted to change for the time being, because they were going to experience the change process in the big picture.

'We are now going to look at our overall financial situation, but we are going to bring our feelings back into it. Only this once, mind you, and only for the purpose of shock therapy.

'I want you to give yourself a financial check-up. Think about your lack of assets, your spending habits, your debt, or whatever gives you a true representation of your financial health. It's important to make pictures of yourself in this state. Try to visualise your material life, your working life and your domestic situation. The things you have, the things you don't have. Get as many pictures into your head as you can. Now let the feelings come. What does it feel like to be in your present state of financial health? Keep your eyes closed and let the pictures work.

'Now I want you to think about something that you're doing or not doing now, or some attitude you have or don't have, that you know is stopping you from getting ahead financially. It could be that you don't stick to your budget, or that you are holding back on a great business idea, or that your life is so cluttered you can't focus on building financial strength. Or it could be impulsive shopping, or binge spending, or low personal productivity, or an expensive addiction. Or maybe it's just psychological — you don't believe you deserve to be rich, or you just feel powerless, or you don't have the courage to take informed risks, or you waste your time dreaming about winning the lottery.

'Now I want you to define this behaviour that you want to change and decide how much you want to change. Remember, it's not about just getting rich. That's not what you want to change. You want to change your inability to do what you say you're going to do, and in this exercise you're going to start with money. In other words, in terms of being true to yourself, what is the one thing you really, really want to change which you know will set you on the path to getting your financial act together? What must you promise yourself to do?'

I let the music run for a while. It was a beautiful piece of slow-moving Baroque music: 60 beats a minute, the perfect rate for a relaxed heartbeat.

'Now I want everyone to take a step forward five years into the future. Imagine what it feels like not to have changed. Fill your mind with pictures: you're still working for that rotten company; you're struggling to meet mortgage repayments; you have precious few savings and you're running on empty: you see a holiday brochure with spectacular views from a villa on a Greek island but you can't afford it; the bills are still hanging over you; perhaps your debt has got worse; imagine yourself saying no to a reasonable request from one of your children because you have no money; perhaps your marriage is feeling the strain, with arguments, recriminations, frustrations. Imagine what it feels like.'

The changes that came over their faces were quite dramatic. It was as if I was looking at a living tableau of worry.

'Now I want you to take another step forward, this time to 10 years into the future. You still haven't changed. You are no further along on the road to financial freedom than you were 10 years ago. Let the pictures take shape. Everything you see and feel spells LOSER to you. How does it feel to be the same as you always were?'

I looked at them one by one. They were obviously all in a private world of imagined, but very possible, disappointment. Their bodies slumped, their breathing was shallow.

'Now another step forward, everyone. We're going 20 years into the future and you're still the same. By now you have given up on your dream. By now it's too late. Think and feel the worst possible scenario. As ugly, as hopeless as you can feel. What have been the consequences of your not changing? What will be the true cost of being the same? How will this ultimately rob you of your life? '

Suddenly, Margaret walked out of the room. She was visibly upset. Oddly enough, none of the others noticed her leaving, not even Mitch.

'Now I want you to take three steps back to where you were, back to the present. When you're ready — there's no rush — open your eyes.' While they were coming back to the present I went out to fetch Margaret. She was having a little weep out in the corridor.

'It's OK,' she said. 'I'm an artist, and I have a very powerful visual sense. It was too much for me. My marriage was over. I could see it all very clearly.'

'Sounds to me like you're on your way to some real change in your life.'

We came back into a room of silence. Not a single happy face.

'We're not finished,' I said. 'It's time to experience the effects of changed behaviour. Take your places again. Now we're going for a completely different ride. This time we will have kept our promises to ourselves and changed our behaviour. Eyes closed. Music.'

We began the same journey again. I asked them to have a clear image of themselves with this new mode of behaviour, and to be as specific as possible. It was entirely up to them to determine what would constitute changed behaviour, but they had to know exactly what they wanted to change and how far they wanted to go with that change. I encouraged them to spend time thinking about their old behaviour — what triggered it, why they wanted to change it, why they had failed in the past, what pressures would be on them to revert to it — and then to think about how different they'd be when they did change, and how their changed behaviour would affect others.

'Remember that real, permanent change, no matter how small, is going to alter the big picture forever.

'Also, take advantage of the feedback of others. Listen to what other people have said to you. We're often ignorant of much of our behaviour and frequently need someone else to point out the obvious, to draw attention to our negative attitudes, our obsessions or our inconsistencies. We can pretend for years that we're not guilty of inappropriate behaviour, until someone we trust shows us all the damning evidence. Welcome it. You need as much evidence as you can gather. You need it to build your case for change, because later on you may need to remind yourself of your reasons.

'While you're in the present, imagine yourself practising, deliberately, consciously, your new behaviour. You're in the *conscious competence* stage, which is the hard work stage. First, choose the change you are going to make — to your spending habits, your financial planning, your budgeting, your revenue streams.

'Your focus should be on learning to be true to your word about changing this behaviour. You're experiencing, perhaps one day at a time, a conquest over the self. You're rediscovering the control you use to govern your behaviour.

'When you think you have completely assimilated your new behaviour and your changed behaviour is working naturally — even automatically — move forward five years. Take your time. Only when you are ready.'

I enjoy this exercise because of the transformation that takes place on the participants' faces. As they moved from five, to 10 to 20 years into the future, visualising and feeling the outcomes of their changed behaviour, their faces beamed with joy. Even conservative Phil and sensitive Margaret seemed transfigured.

'You are now living in the Rich Matrix. You're no longer aware of any learning process. The disruption is over; your new behaviour is now the norm. You have mastered your life, made your money, and are enjoying the fruits of self-mastery.'

They stayed in their trance-like state for several minutes, listening to the music, enjoying a foretaste, albeit only imagined, of financial freedom.

There was nothing further to be said.

6. The authenticity filter

Frustration results from a lot of effort producing no return. Bitching is a sign of frustration, and frustration is a symptom of inauthentic living.

'**I**'m getting frustrated.' Margaret telephoned me to say. 'You still haven't told us how to grow rich.'

'It's simple. Just stop being frustrated,' I said.

'Toney, cut the riddles. What the hell does that mean?'

'See you in class, Margaret.'

I have a very simple belief about what causes frustration in life. Frustration results from a lot of effort producing no return. Frustration with one's life therefore results from doing the wrong thing with one's life. Similarly, frustration with one's financial life results from doing the wrong thing with one's money.

The solution is even simpler: identify the right thing to do and do it.

I believe that finding out what is the right thing to do is a question of identifying what requires the least effort for the greatest return. That is, after all, the principle of smart investment.

Logically, what requires the least effort is that which flows most naturally from a person's authentic self.

Since authenticity is the harmony between what a person is and what he or she does, acting authentically — or naturally and effortlessly — is therefore the answer to frustration.

Few of us would dare admit the many things we've done that could just as well not have been done for all the good they did. So much of what we do, and have done, has little to do with who we are, and does not contribute one iota to our growth as human beings, which is not very smart investment thinking. How long would you stick to an investment strategy if there was no return on it?

We've also been told that every experience makes us richer. Life's tapestry and all that. That would be fine if we lived a thousand years, but in the context of life being short, it's just plain twaddle. Some experiences in life are valuable, and therefore enriching, but most are trivial and therefore forgettable. Much of what we do has nothing to do with who we are, and gives precious little return on our investment of time and effort. No wonder we feel frustrated.

Moreover, since life is short, a person's financial life, the time he or she has to make money, is much shorter — this should give us all a sense of great urgency. Getting no return for the effort we put into our financial life is a source of serious frustration. Think of the number of years you've spent working hard and how little you have to show for it, think of how you've been expending considerable energy just treading water to keep yourself from drowning. A good deal of the sound and fury of your financial past has probably amounted to not much more than keeping you afloat, marking time until something comes over the horizon.

If getting your financial life right is a matter of urgency, why are you marking time? Wouldn't it be much more sensible to choose to do what requires the least effort for the greatest return? Wouldn't it be much better, in other words, to act authentically?

In an abundant world, where there's plenty for everyone, we have the luxury of reasonable waste. But there is one thing which we should never waste, and that is *time*.

That the rich are rich because they never waste a penny is a silly myth for which there is little evidence. People do not become rich by being misers. Miserly people have one thing in common whether they wear suits or rags, live in a mansion or on the streets: they are not truly rich, because they are not truly free.

That the truly rich do not waste their *time* doing that which returns very little, however, is a proposition for which there is overwhelming evidence.

The object of this session was to teach my students that to grow rich they had to learn to distinguish between a good investment of time and effort and a bad one. Most people believe that you do this through goal setting and time management. I believe that you do it by knowing what is authentically you — identifying your defining talent — and then letting the goals establish themselves naturally.

The theme of the class was straightforward: if what you do is inauthentic, if it does not flow naturally from you, you're headed for a life of frustration. On the other hand, if what you do is authentic in the sense that it comes easily and naturally to you, you're headed for a full and productive life with maximum return.

I started the session with some observations on wasted time and effort.

'Has your bitching about not being rich ever helped you realise yourself? Has it ever helped you develop your full potential? Apart from the comfort of self-pity, what does bitching about life really have to do with your growth as a human being? What does it do? What returns on your time and effort has it produced?'

Their answers were as quick as they were obvious.

'It keeps Mitch in fail mode. Stops him from believing in himself.'

'It's preventing Margaret from believing in him too. And that means it's breaking up their marriage.' Margaret never minced her words.

'It saps Phil's energy. His taxi passengers do it all the time, so by the time he ends his shift, he's totally drained.'

'It blinds Leon to possibility. Half his day is spent thinking about everything that's going wrong.'

'What you have just done is produce some solid evidence of inauthentic living,' I said. 'Bitching doesn't advance your life one bit, does it? There is no return on your investment of time and effort. Not like other things you do. You learn to drive because that makes you mobile. You go on a course to advance your career because that will fulfil you. You eat because your body needs food to function. You make love because, among other things, it's a biological necessity. But bitching about not being rich? How does it help you move forward?

'Bitching, however, is also an expression of your frustration with life. It's a sign that you're spending your time on what doesn't matter instead of what does; using it up on the dross instead of the dream.

'To sort out the dross from the dream you need a filter; a kind of personal sieve that can separate what really matters to you from what doesn't. That filter — used for deciding the best investment of your time and effort — is your authenticity.

> Authenticity is the harmony between being and doing. We instinctively know who we are and who we are not.

'Authenticity is the harmony between who you are and what you do. It's the consistency between being and doing, between your essence and the life you lead. It's when what you do flows naturally from who you are.

'So are you leading an authentic life? A shotgun question, perhaps, but if you ask it seriously enough, it'll reverberate for years.'

'Obviously not,' Margaret said acidly, 'or we wouldn't be here. And anyway, you can only act authentically if you know who you are.'

'Right,' I said. 'But you *do* know who you are. We all know who we are and who we are not — *instinctively*.'

I explained that knowing who you are is intuitive. The fact that you can't put it into a few sentences doesn't matter; it's something you know instinctively, not something you can argue yourself into.

Your essence is your authentic self; it's what makes you unique.

'We could also talk about your authentic self as your essence, which is yours, unique and incontrovertible. It's everything that makes your existence particular. It makes you, and makes you different from the other six billion people on the Earth. You can choose to thwart or nurture your essence, but you can't fundamentally change it.

'You know your essence. You have more than a nodding acquaintance with it, more than a mere working knowledge of it. You know yourself instinctively and certainly, better than anyone else does. No one, absolutely no one, will know your essence better than you. Ever.'

After sitting through hundreds of sessions listening to people attempt to define who they are, I'm now convinced that the whole exercise is futile. Language can't cope with such a demand; it'll always fall short of articulating, with any degree of useful precision, a complex individual. That is why I have stopped relying exclusively on personality profiling, psychometric testing, or any of the professional tools used to describe people. They often come up only with approximate generalisations about the person. Sometimes they even mask it.

You know who you are. If you didn't, you'd have absolutely no reference in your life for your thoughts, words, deeds and omissions. In fact, without this knowledge you couldn't make conscious choices.

This self-knowledge can't be taken away from you. You can lose absolutely everything in the world, but your self-knowledge is yours to keep.

There's another piece of tacit knowledge that's just as important as knowing who you are, and that is knowing who you're not. Think of the times you have felt that you were not being you. You can probably recall a thousand situations in which you knew you were not being you. Haven't you said those words — 'It's just not me' — more times than you can count?

> You know who you are and who you're not.

'Grace can remember getting jealous because her boyfriend had the hots for another girl. She threw his laptop at him and walked out in a huff. That's not her. She usually doesn't lose it like that,' Grace volunteered

'At the staff Christmas party Andy got really drunk and went over the top. He said things that just weren't him. Then he spent a week going around the office apologising and trying to explain that he was not really like that.'

'Leon remembers that. It was definitely not Andy.'

'All these times when you've behaved or spoken in a way that just wasn't you, you may not have known why, but you did know that it just wasn't you. Something was misplaced, out of kilter; it was as if someone else were acting and speaking on your behalf. You sensed the fundamental wrongness of it. In other words, in those moments you knew, instinctively and certainly, who you were not.

'Authenticity is therefore two-sided: you know who you are and you know who you aren't. That you can't put it into words, write an autobiography or proclaim it in a public forum isn't the point. It's tacit knowledge, which is just as important and useful as explicit knowledge.

'Understanding authenticity begins with accepting that you know who you are and who you're not. Don't listen to all the flimflam about identity metaphors and the like. It's academic, self-indulgent and ultimately fruitless; just more of the pointless self-analysis we use to compose interesting stories about ourselves. But we're not fiction.

> Self-analysis often just results in another story; it's better to trust your instinctive self-knowledge.

We're fact, and some facts, such as your own indisputable self-knowledge, though instinctive and unexpressed, are powerful tools.

'It's actually a great relief when you stop trying to define who you are, when you stop playing games with this instinctive, natural, pure knowledge, and just be who you are and do what you do naturally. Trust your self-knowledge; it's what successful people do.

'If, on the other hand, you don't use this instinctive self-knowledge to live with authenticity, you may never be free of frustration.

'Without being unnecessarily alarmist, imagine the final horror of "I could have, and I knew I could have, but I didn't." Fast-forward yourself 30 years, turn around to face your life and feel how those words would sound. I wouldn't wish them on anyone, because in the twilight of your life "I could have" would only signal profound, irremediable disappointment. It's not about the dream you didn't live out, a career you didn't follow or a skill you didn't learn. It's much, much deeper than that. You're asking yourself what it would have been like if you had done what you could have done, been what you could have been; if you had just let the knowledge of who you are be the absolute measure of what you do.

'Think about having a knack for something, something that comes from your essence, a natural fitness for something, and for one reason or another just ignoring it. How disappointed would you feel knowing you had an amazing talent you just let die — simply because you chose to ignore your natural ability, or you recognised it too late, or you just didn't trust it. Or even more significantly, you were too frightened to surrender to it.

> Think of the horror of admitting, at the end of your life, that you could have been you but you weren't.

'Try to say these words. "I could have been me, but I wasn't." Don't they sound just awful?

'Of course it's not always easy to identify our natural gifts. Some people do it early. Others set their life goals without ever doing it and then spend most of their life frustrated.

'But those living in the Rich Matrix have found it. They make money because what they do to make that money is authentically connected to who they are. In other words, they act authentically because what they do is what they do best.

> The rich do what they do best.

'There you have it; one of the clues to getting rich — do what you do best. In other words, be authentic.

'Imagine the difference to your life if you could feel with absolute clarity and conviction that what you're doing is what you do best, that what you produce comes naturally from your essence. Imagine the feeling of effortless performance, of knowing that what you do is right because it "feels" right; it fits you perfectly, suits you and is you.

'So this much we know to be true: If what we do and how we live doesn't proceed naturally from our essence, which we know instinctively and certainly, we can expect some serious frustration with life. But if it does, then we're in for a lot of joy — and wealth.'

'People in the Rich Matrix love what they do because it's what they do best. If you don't love what you do, consider doing something more attuned to who you really are.

'I still don't get,' Cathy said. 'How do we know if what we're doing flows naturally from who we are?'

'Well, ask yourself if you love what you spend most of your day doing. A show of hands, please. Who is not happy in the work they do?'

All hands went up, except Cathy's.

'Except for Cathy, the rest of you are not enjoying what you spend a third of your life doing. Of course it may not be practical just to strike camp and go walkabout. But the long-term alternative is not attractive, because if you can't say you love what you do, the chances of your bitching for the rest of your life are fairly high.

'And even if you love what you do, as Cathy does, is it what you do best? If it isn't, if what you spend a third of your life doing isn't a genuine expression of your natural ability, then at some stage the pain of frustration will hit.

'If what you're doing isn't what you love doing most, what you just can't help doing, that which absorbs your total self, there will be a price to pay.

'So many people are in jobs unsuited to their natures, on wealth creation plans that are unrelated to their real selves or in relationships that don't allow them to truly express themselves, because they won't make choices using their instinctive self-knowledge — their authenticity filter.'

'But Toney, Cathy doesn't know what she does best,' Cathy said.

'Just because you haven't found it yet, it doesn't mean you won't find it. You might try a thousand things that just aren't you, but one day you'll hit upon something that's totally and unequivocally you. You'll know it instinctively and certainly. Then you can choose to go for it or not. That's when you're on your way to making money.

'I'm not suggesting that you suddenly get up and walk out of whatever you're doing. One day you may have to do that, but not all transitions need to be revolutions. Begin by trusting your instinctive knowledge about yourself and take it from there. If you already know what makes you feel who you really are, just do it. It'll make you exceptional in whatever you choose to do, whether it's makes you money or not. Doing the thing that defines you, even if no one wants to pay you for it, is still the best recipe I know for happiness.

'Let's think about what inspires us when we see exceptional people living authentic lives. When we watch the Olympics, a gathering of some of the most physically talented people in the world, we're eyewitnesses to excellence in its purest form: thousands of accomplished people doing what they do best, with extraordinary results. The professional diver propelling himself through a perfect parabola or the basketball player leaping to shoot and score a magnificent three-pointer are doing what they do best. Similarly, the singer filling an auditorium with the magnificent sound of pure music, the stockmarket trader with uncanny insight into the movement of markets, and the surgeon in ten hours of pure focus all excel because they're doing what they do best. But it's not just the skills that excite us. We can be in awe of them or admire how they've been perfected. We can recognise the years of discipline and sacrifice and effort required to become one of the greats. But these alone do not thrill us. What really thrills us is the combination of learned skill and natural ability coming together in an act of excellence.

> Excellence is possible when you love what you do, and it's what you do best.

'The Rich often work hard, but since they love what they do and it's what they do best, there is harmony between who they are and what they do. In other words, excellence flows from the fact that you are doing what is really you.

'Everyone has a defining ability, something that they naturally do well, something that inspires them, that they love doing because it's "so them". Very often, this thing will make them lots of money. My guess is you probably already know what is indisputably you.

'Of the people I have met who exist in the Bitch Matrix, most admit to being frustrated with their lives in some way. As we have seen, the principal cause of frustration lies in inauthentic living — when there's discordance between a person's life and what they naturally do best. Something isn't quite right; they're out of alignment.'

'You can't just start living authentically, just like that, can you?' Leon asked.

'No, but you can make it an issue in your life. You can start by getting into the habit of questioning what you're doing: "Is what I'm doing at the moment authentic? Is it in accord with who I am, what I love doing and what I do best?"

'So, is it? Is your work really you? Does it fulfil you? Or are you frustrated because it just doesn't flow naturally from who you are?

'You know yourself, so you know if your present employment proceeds from your essence. You know if it is what you love doing. You know if it's authentic. And you know if it's just about paying the rent and getting by.'

'Toney, you can't tell people to leave their jobs!!' Margaret nearly leaped from her seat. 'It's not that easy.'

'Of course it's not easy. It's much easier just to coast along and hope something turns up. But if you have the guts to leave your job, you've probably got what it takes to grow rich.

'Our conclusion, then, is simple. If your present work isn't really you — and I suspect for most of you it isn't — you're not being true to yourself. You're living an inauthentic life. You will never build real wealth until you make a radical change.

'But not until you're ready. I don't want you all to go home and quit tonight. All I am suggesting is that you ask yourself honestly if what you are doing with your life is what you love doing and what you do best. If it isn't, you know the consequences.

'Not much of a choice is it? Fulfilment or frustration?'

Isn't it strange that so few people have the courage to choose what obviously brings them the most happiness?

7. The really, really recipe

To achieve what you want requires really wanting it.

The main reason we break our promises to ourselves is that we didn't really make them in the first place. This is because we often don't know what we *really, really* want. We either want everything, or we want so vaguely that we can't narrow it down to something achievable. We have no clear desire which can generate a driving, single-minded, zero-option passion. Sadly, *without* such clarity of purpose, we will be forever floundering in mediocrity. Happily, *with* it, we will be unstoppable.

You can, of course, want mediocrity. You can be happy being a 'have-not', or a 'will-have'. It's easy. It's a life without risk or danger; there's no need to deal with the unexpected in a life that is as predictable one day as the next. To me, however, such a life amounts to no life.

The rich don't make money in a vacuum; they make it because what they want is clearly defined in space and time. Their dreams, the changes they want in their lives, are anchored in reality. They have a clear understanding

Life has no time for 'tyre-kickers'.

of how much, how and by when. This clarity of desire allows them to focus their passion and excel.

We were now moving into our seventh week. It was the most crucial week of the course, because it was time to throw out some serious challenges to the group. I was determined that this course was going to be life-changing; it was not going to be just a set of lectures which floated off like party balloons. Over and over again I had been stressing how important it was to be serious about change. Now the time had come to show my students just how serious they had to be.

Unfortunately, this would mean that some of my students would leave the course. They would not leave because they wanted to; I would ask them to. There is no point attending change programs, reading books on personal growth, spending hours with a lifestyle coach, unless you are serious about doing something. It's like learning a foreign language you will never use or toying with a career 'just for fun'. Life is brief. There is no time to be a 'tyre-kicker', someone who just wants to look and has no serious intention to commit. There is no time to waste; no time to play Bridget Jones. It's real, permanent change or it's nothing.

When the students arrived, I handed a postcard to each of them.

'The first thing I want you to do is address this postcard to yourself.'

'You are only going to get one go at writing on this postcard, one go for the answer to the most important question in your life at the moment: What do you really, really want? What is it that you want more than anything else in the world?

'There will be no second attempts at what you put on that postcard, no going back on what you *really, really* want. Just one thing: a change, a new habit, an amount of money, a job, a business, a partner, a home.

> Sentence yourself to what you really want. And make it a life sentence.

Whatever it is, it must be specific. It is no good saying, "I want to be rich" or "I want to be financially independent", "I want love", "I want security" or "I want health". Such statements will leave you in the same limbo you started this course in.

> Take time to define what you want in life, before you run out of time.

'By the end of the next session, you will have written one sentence on that self-addressed postcard. It's not a mission statement or a vision statement. I call it a "life sentence": it sentences you in a positive way to serve time on the most important thing you want in your life.

'When you return for the next session, I will ask for everyone's postcard. If you cannot clarify what you *really, really* want exactly, and commit to it 100 per cent honestly, I will ask you to leave the course. If you are not sure, I will also ask you to leave and to come back another day, when you are sure. So write on the postcard exactly what you want, how much of it you want, how you are going to get it, when you are going to get it, and where you are going to get it. All in one sentence.

'I will post these cards to you so that they arrive on the day you have specified. For instance, if you want to start your own business by the end of November, you will receive your postcard at the end of the November. If what you want will take you three years to achieve, you will receive it exactly three years from now.

'The postcard will call you to account, so whatever you want has to be achievable and realistic. This isn't a class exercise. It's not an assignment. It's a deadly serious promise that has to be honoured without compromise. Nothing is more important — I repeat — nothing is more important than keeping yourself focused on what you write on that postcard. If you're not

> When it comes to what is really important in life, there is no such thing as changing your mind.

prepared to take up this challenge, you have no reason to be here. The time for playing games is over. You're no longer wishing upon a star, throwing a coin into a fountain, or dreaming of Lady Luck; you're taking your life into your own hands.'

I waited for a minute. I must have been wearing my best deadly serious look, because there wasn't a sound in the room. Even Margaret looked impressed. 'Any questions?'

'It's impossible, Toney. Cathy has no idea what she wants. She's never had any idea. How can she decide this in a week?' Cathy asked.

'What has Cathy got on tomorrow night?'

'She's been invited to dinner by some friends.'

'If Cathy is serious about life, she will cancel it. She will cancel absolutely everything until she has come up with a positive life sentence.'

'She can't cancel an invitation just like that!'

'Then Cathy doesn't understand what I mean by saying that nothing is more important than what she is about to do. If Cathy wants to go any further on this journey, this must be her priority. I don't care if she stays in bed thinking about it all week, or if she goes off on a mountain retreat. Whatever it takes. A week of suspended life in which she determines a new direction for her life will be one of the most significant weeks of her life.'

'But what if Mitch changes his mind?'

'Once Mitch writes his life sentence down on that postcard, that's it. This is zero-option thinking. There is no such thing as changing one's mind.'

'And if we can't come up with anything?'

'Then, for your own sake, do not come back next week. In fact, if you don't arrive at something to which you can commit yourself with unswerving focus, I will ask you to leave. You are wasting your time. I know this is harsh, but it is the only way to move forward.

> Do you want to be happy or not? Is there a simpler question?

'You're all probably thinking I'm oversimplifying things; that you are all much more complicated than a single sentence. I say that's just more blah-blah. It's just another ruse of the mind to run away from the effort of self-actualisation. Being miserable or happy is a simple choice: if you want to be miserable, deeply disappointed in life, live the life you don't want; if you want to be happy, deeply happy in life, live the life you want.'

'It can't be that simple,' Margaret said. 'If it were, we wouldn't be here.'

'But it is. It's a simple enough question: What do you *really, really* want more than anything in the world? What is the one passion that would drive you to the ends of the earth? Actually, I think we complicate the question because we're actually scared of the answer.'

'Andy is not scared of the answer; he's just scared he won't be able to make the answer a reality.'

'If it's not achievable, then it's not what Andy *really, really* wants. Don't confuse fantasy, such as being the majority shareholder in the world's largest company, with wanting what is both possible and probable, such as creating a self-generating income for the rest of your life. One is irrational and therefore unachievable and can only be wanted in a flight of fantasy. The other is rational and can be *really, really* wanted on the basis of real *facts*, real *probabilities* and real *possibilities*.'

> What you want in life must be based on the facts of your life and the possibility and probability of it happening.

I turned to the whiteboard and wrote:

FACTS, POSSIBILITIES, PROBABILITIES

'These are the first ingredients of the *really, really* recipe. But a word of caution; the possible is not the same as the imaginable. I might imagine myself as the front row forward for the Australian National Rugby League team, but given my size, my age and my lack of training, it is impossible, no matter how imaginable it is.

'Whenever I hear people say you can be whoever you want to be, I feel like screaming — "But not whoever you *imagine* yourself to be." What you want must be based on the facts of your life, on what is possible and what, as a result of your efforts, is probable.' I paused for a minute to let it sink in.

> If it's not achievable, it's fantasy and will only bring disappointment.

'So when we say *really, really*, we will now think facts, possibilities and probabilities. Does anyone know what else goes into the recipe?'

'Enthusiasm,' Phil said from the back of the room.

'Exactly.' I turned to the whiteboard and wrote *Passion*.

'But we're not talking about shrieking, boisterous passion. You don't have to gyrate to the sound of primal screaming or burst a blood vessel to be

> 'Whatever your hand finds to do, do it with all your might.'
> Ecclesiastes 9:11

passionate. We're talking about a steely, self-fuelled determination that brings with it, quietly or sometimes explosively, the power to live the life you really, really want.

'Passion is not noise. It's the power that comes with being right, absolutely, unquestionably right, because you know that what you're doing is what you really want to do — it's based on facts, it's possible and it's probable. So what about making money? Do you really, really want to get rich? More than anything else in the world?'

> Real passion comes from knowing you are doing what you really want to do, and real passion is a prelude to real getting.

'At the moment, that's what Mitch needs.'

'I didn't say "need", I said "want". Everyone needs more money but it's only those who really, really want it who get it. Suppose I offered Andy $1 million for every successive day he made $100 more than the previous day. Would he do it?'

'Of course,' Andy said. 'Get out your cheque book.'

I laughed. 'Think about it seriously. After three months, not only would Andy have his life back, and all the money he made, but he'd also have an extra $90 million to spend. He'd really want it if he knew the return was going to be so high. He would be passionate about it because the pleasure of never having to worry about money again would be far greater than the pain of working for it. Can anyone tell me what I am trying to say?'

'People make money because they passionately want to,' Grace said.

'Spot on. Passionately wanting is a prelude to really getting. Some people will go to any lengths to be with the person they love, because they really, really want to. Some people will go mad in a gym because, for them, a body to die for is something they would almost die for.

'So walk out this door and don't return until you really, really want something more than anything else in the world. Whatever it is — money, a trip to the Antarctic, a recording contract — it must be specific. What we're learning here is completely worthless unless you know what you *really, really* want. So are all the courses you go on, the tapes you listen to, the gurus whose books you read.'

I could see Leon thinking hard.

'Does Leon have a question?'

'How does Leon get passion? How do you make passion?'

'Aha! The solution is not to manufacture passion. You can't try to *make* getting rich something you want to do more than anything else in the

> Passion is not manufactured; it flows from our greatest values and our greatest talents.

world. And you can't pretend to yourself that you *really, really* want to get rich, because your intending self would always be in conflict with your behaving self. So if you don't *really, really* want to get rich, you're wasting your time trying to; anything you do will be undermined by your intending self. If you do *really, really* want to get rich, and that want is in alignment with your strongest value, you'll find the passion to act on your want.'

It was getting a bit complicated. Time for another example. 'Grace, tell me one thing that Grace really wants.'

'Grace wants to lose ten kilos.'

'Good. The *really, really* principle works with weight management. The *facts* are — pardon me, Grace — she is 10 kilos overweight. It is *possible* for her to lose that. It is *probable* that if she set out on a weight management program she would lose the weight. All she needs now is the *passion*. If she *really, really* wants to be thin, if she wants it more than anything else in the world, she won't go anywhere near a cream-filled pastry. I bet the reason Grace struggles with binge dieting and seasonal reform is that she doesn't *really, really* want to lose that weight. She might think she wants to, but she doesn't *really, really* want to do it. I suggest she is missing passion.'

> To really want is to want it more than anything else in the world.

'But she does *really, really* want to,' she said. 'She thinks about it all the time.'

'Thinking about something all the time is not the same as really wanting it. Let me show you what *really, really* wanting is about. Imagine a surgeon coming up to you in your hospital bed and saying, "I refuse to save your life unless you lose a third of your body weight." You'd then want it more

> Thinking about something constantly is an act of the mind; it is not the same as really wanting it, which is an act of the whole self.

than anything else in the world, and you would have the passion to do it, because it would be a matter of life or death. This would create natural, real passion.

'Compare this passion with what happens, for example, when you read a corporate mission statement. I have observed many trainers in the workplace trying to stir up passion for corporate goals. It simply doesn't work unless the passion works from the inside out, unless those involved *really, really* want to commit, unless it's unquestionably real to them. If your commitment to change is as impersonal as your commitment to a corporate goal, you won't get far.

> You act with passion when you act in line with what is most important in your life.

'Like everyone else, I've vowed commitment to corporate mission statements when, deep down, it was just show. It wasn't what I *really, really* wanted. I'd be some sorry person if my tombstone read, "He helped increase the market share of Piddly-Poo Nappies", when what I *really, really* wanted was a rewarding job, respect, fulfilment and enjoyment in the workplace.

'You act with passion when you live according to your values — what you hold to be most important in your life. Your values, your strongest desires, will generate the passion needed to live by them.'

> The master want of a human being is to be master of the self.

'What about wanting to be happy more than anything else in the world?

'Can anyone answer Cathy's question?'

'Wanting to be happy is too vague. You couldn't sustain daily passion for that,' Phil said. Phil was turning into my star pupil.

'Well then, let's ask Cathy what would make her happy.'

'Cathy knows. She wants to be able to do what you were talking about the other night. She wants to keep her promises to herself. She wants to obey herself. That would make her happy, because then she would achieve what she set out to do.'

'Is that something Cathy could be passionate about? Is that something Cathy could become obsessed by?'

'You bet,' Cathy said, wide-eyed as ever.

'I think Cathy is onto a source of happiness all of you would probably agree on. Imagine reaching the end of your life knowing that you had fulfilled yourself by being true to your word; that you had never betrayed yourself; that you had taken your life into your own hands; that action had always made good your commitment; that when you had said you loved someone, you did, and when you had said you would change, you did. Imagine it. Courage, strength of conviction, the sense of a life fully lived, all coming together as a final comment on your life. Wouldn't that be wonderful?'

I turned to the whiteboard again and wrote the next ingredient of the *really, really* recipe:

OPTIMISM.

'Have you noticed that living in the Bitch Matrix drains your energy? It is no wonder you can't find the passion to go after what you really, really want, when your energy is being wasted on bitching about life.

'Optimism, on the other hand, will generate the energy you need to be passionate about what you really, really want.

> Optimism generates passion

'The depth and extent of your passion is controlled by your attitude. Now I know you've probably had a gutful of people — especially me — telling you that your attitude sucks. You've said it yourselves. You've been living in the Bitch Matrix with the Bitch Attitude for years. So was I. So do millions of other people.

> Your attitude will set the limits of your action.

'However, your attitude is not set in stone. You can swap your disempowering attitude for a positive empowering one. Take your attitude to this course as an example. I know sometimes you find it all a bit much, and sometimes your attention flags. But if you don't approach change with a zealous, even over-the-top, attitude, you can expect very limited results.

> There is only a one-letter difference between attitude and aptitude.

'We have learned that the rich are in control of their lives because they bring about change, and they do that by keeping the promises they make themselves and being true to themselves. This is the main theme of our journey. Those in the Rich Matrix differ from those in the Bitch Matrix in another fundamental way: their attitude to change.

'It's such a pity the expression "you've got an attitude" carries a negative connotation in modern usage, because if you want to get what you really, really want then you must have a powerful, positive attitude. It's not just the backdrop to the change you seek; it's the actual force behind it, providing real momentum to your efforts. How well you succeed in changing your behaviour depends on this.

'The Rich Matrix attitude generates energy; the Bitch Matrix attitude just wastes it. The Rich Matrix attitude makes learning new behaviour possible; the Bitch Matrix attitude just blocks it. In other words, the rich love life — not because they have money, but because they have a life-affirming attitude that makes them open to making money and the changes that extra money will bring to their lives. Those who bitch about life do so not just because they have no money, but because they have a fundamentally life-denying attitude that closes them to making money and the possible changes that money would bring.

'Attitude makes a big difference. You can't do anything well if you hate doing it. Think back to your school days, when your attitude to a subject rather than your intellectual ability

> To bring about real change, you have to have a positive attitude.

determined your progress. A teacher with the wrong chemistry, an irrational "block" against a subject, an enemy in the class or just the boring way the material was presented probably marred your interest in, and therefore knowledge of, a particular subject for life. How different would your experience of that subject have been had your attitude been different? Wouldn't you have been able to improve your scores if you had known how to change your attitude?

'The same is true for personal growth. You're not going to get out of the Bitch Matrix if there's a great "inner yawn" going on, because to bring about change, to experience *metanoia*, you have to be fired up. You have to be filled with an enthusiasm almost bordering on mania. You must thrill to the thought of daily challenge and triumph.

'If it's not going to make a difference to your life, why are you wasting your time with it? If you doubt you have the right attitude, think seriously before you undertake this program of change; you'll

> If what you're doing is not really important, why are you doing it?

probably be wasting your time.

'If you're going to hate the process, don't bother starting, because you're not going to get far. Unless you're excited about the change, you're probably going to last one or two weeks and then give up; you'll have no staying power. If you approach the change process with a running negative commentary — it's going to be tough, a struggle uphill all the way — you'll make it exactly that. This kind of negative attitude will be self-fulfilling.

'On the other hand, if you use all the power within you, going full-speed ahead with your imagination, deploying the entire range of your sensory mechanisms to view and experience the change process as fun, inspiring, challenging and achievable, you're already halfway there.

'Just realising you have this power to change should generate a winner's attitude. And when you do win, and you're the primary agent of change, the win is so much more exhilarating.

> Your attitude determines your altitude.

'"My life in my own hands" is the ultimate thrill, the buzz of being alive. Experiencing the benefits of a change you have brought about yourself, by tapping into your own resources, is one of the greatest personal highs you'll ever have.

'So you have to enjoy the changeover from Bitch Matrix to Rich Matrix. It's an odd thing to say, "You have to enjoy", but if you don't get a thrill out of going after your goals, you're just making it harder to reach them. If, however, you love the feeling of going forward, putting your body and mind behind your decision, combining all your strengths into a single direction, then metanoia is more than probable — it's certain.

'It's no good sitting in a room and dispassionately saying to yourself, "I'm going to lose weight", or, "I'm going to focus on building my family", or, "I feel positive". If your heart isn't in it, it doesn't matter how often you repeat affirmations — you've already made them ineffective. Your limit is set by your attitude. If you commit to change with the right attitude — the zero-option power — plus passion, zeal you can feel, and honest and authentic enthusiasm from the centre of yourself, you'll get there.

> Metanoia is rooted in a passionate love of change.

'You need total involvement. You don't score from the sidelines; you must be in the game, involved in every minute of the change process, directing your own progress, fuelling your own motion.

'Radical change requires an unconditional approach. This is especially so with metanoic decisions, where we change a fundamental belief about the world or ourselves. We need blinkers to keep us focused on our decisions and to sustain our commitment — we are making zero-option decisions, involving uncompromising passion and unshakeable belief.'

I was on fire. The room was on fire.

'You're rockin', Toney,' Andy shouted.

I laughed and turned to write the final ingredient of the *really, really* recipe: *Zero options*.

'Alternatives don't help at all. They rob you of a lot of the power you need. If, for instance, you attempt a radical change such as an end to impulse buying, but keep the thought in the back of your mind that "Well, if this fails, I'll just try again ...", you've already weakened your resolve and undone half your effort.

> The path to failure is littered with contingency plans.

'A zero-option strategy guarantees that you'll achieve what you set out to do, because there's no other option. So you must never plant in your mind the possibility of failure. Don't even have a contingency plan. While a backup plan might seem to be a very sensible thing to do, it actually provides you with a reason not to give 100 per cent of yourself to your project. With a contingency plan, you're telling yourself there is an alternative to reaching your goal of radical change. There isn't. Or rather there is one: the only alternative to reaching your goal of financial freedom is *not* reaching your goal of financial freedom, in which case, why bother in the first place? You'll never succeed if you're prepared to defend yourself with the consolation that "mistakes are understandable". Mistakes are options which will rob your decisions of their power; how understandable they are is immaterial.

'Arrival is about all or nothing. It tolerates neither degrees nor options. Such intolerance is a major source of power; a great weapon against our own mediocrity.

'Why do we accept mediocrity when we know we're capable of moving forward in leaps and bounds, sometimes even towards great wealth and success? If called on to do so, we would risk our lives for the right cause or unthinkingly cross a threshold level of personal strength just to survive. We know that somewhere inside us is the ability to perform truly remarkable acts of courage and self-denial. Yet we stop short of many simple, unheroic goals. Why? Why do we succumb to mediocrity, to the comfort of going nowhere in particular? Why do we break our resolutions and promises? Where did this sense of powerlessness come from? What's wrong with us? Why do we expect so little from ourselves? Few of us will ever be tested by fire or asked to demonstrate superhuman strength. Few of us will be asked to drag a wounded friend across a minefield or be expected to endure torture. They are acts of real heroism.

> Who knows the threshold of their own personal strength?

'There's something wrong with our perspective, isn't there? We're asking ourselves to change a few bad habits that have to do with money and we just can't seem to do it! While others can risk their lives for causes they believe in, we can't say no to a budget-bust or spend a few hours a week reviewing our wealth-making strategies. Have we somehow been deprived of willpower? Where did we learn our helplessness? Are only a few of us allowed to achieve self-mastery?

> We fail because we give ourselves the option of failing.

'The answer to these questions, to our own falling short of the mark, is staring us in the face. We stop short of carrying out our decisions because we give ourselves the option of stopping short. We fail because we give ourselves the option of failing. In other words, options, alternatives and contingency plans are a hindrance to us — so dump them.

'And how will you know you have eradicated options? How will you know your decision is a zero-option one? You'll know it is when you feel it in the pit of your stomach. *Metanoia* hurts. There's effort and sacrifice ahead, without the consolation of options, without the solace of excuse.

'To arrive, to move from current reality to your desired reality, you must be blind to options. And zero-option commitment is about as blind as you get. It implies that if you really want to alter your behaviour, you can, provided you're prepared to go to the extreme, if necessary. You're a human being endowed with a mind so powerful that, when pushed far enough, can make you do things you'd have thought were way out of range. No matter how old you are or how prejudiced against yourself you are, you're capable of fundamental and lasting change. You don't have to be a saint or a soldier to do it. You just have to be yourself, with the single-mindedness of a saint or a soldier. In other words, you have to be of no other mind once your mind is set.'

> 'Try? There is no try. There is only do or not do.'
> Yoda, Star Wars: The Empire Strikes Back

'If you act with zero-option commitment, you're deliberately taking away your freedom to choose any other path but the one leading towards your goal. Such commitment is real liberation, because you're replacing the freedom of options with an even greater freedom: freedom from failure.'

> Only those who are never free to fail are truly free from failure.

I nearly collapsed in exhaustion. It was a session to which I had given everything. As I watched the class sitting there in silence, wondering if they were about to clap or just breathe a sigh of relief, I realised, with absolute certainty, that there had been a breakthrough.

8. Newton's laws for growing rich

> Doing nothing is a sure way to being nothing.

Question: What does a program about getting rich and the teachings of Sir Isaac Newton have in common?

Answer: They both tackle the problem of inertia — the state of bodies at rest, doing nothing.

The great English physicist proposed three laws of motion that have been used since the 17th century to explain the relationship between force, mass and acceleration. Although he would probably do cartwheels in his grave if he knew, his principles are also applicable to the sort of human change management needed to leave the Bitch Matrix and move over to the Rich Matrix. This too is about motion, about moving from one state to another in a specific direction and under the influence of a net force.

Inertia is a real problem. We can talk about passion and attitude, vision and values, but what good does any of that do if, when we know we are ready to change, we actually do nothing? It is a complex problem. There are as many reasons why people fail to take action as there are different personalities, and the literature on personal inertia throws up a battery of such reasons, drawn from disciplines as diverse as psychology, biology, sociology, education and even astrology. All of these are for the most part convincing, but few of them apply universally, alas.

I have often thought that if we could find a few simple rules to move us to action, self-mastery would become no more difficult than a game of football. You get the ball and you do something

> The best way to unplug what's blocking you is to pull your finger out.

with it. Sadly, it's not like that. Too often we get the ball and then do nothing with it. In mid-field, with strategies uppermost in our mind, our self-knowledge ready for action and the goalposts in sight, all we do is stand there, like lifeless dummies, holding the ball. Before long we're tackled, and our chance has passed.

I think that 80 per cent of the problem is solved using the '*really, really* want' formula. If you *really, really* want to do something then you are on your way to doing that. The reverse is true. Not *really, really* wanting to do something can be the real reason behind our inertia, our procrastination and our wavering commitment.

The other 20 per cent of the problem is solved by the fundamental laws of physics.

There's nothing really complicated about Newton's three laws of motion; we experience them in everything we do.

Newton's first law states that an object at rest remains at rest unless acted upon by an outside force, and an object in motion continues to move in a straight

> Inertia is a complicated problem with a simple answer: do something.

line in the same direction unless an outside force acts upon it. A ball will stay still, or continue to move in a straight line at a constant velocity in the same direction, unless a force acts upon it. If it's moving, it will only swerve or stop when friction or some other force is applied to it. Otherwise, it will (theoretically) continue forever at the same velocity in a straight line in the same direction.

Human behaviour works in exactly the same way. No amount of hoping for change will make it happen. To change one's behaviour, a force must be applied. An effort must be exerted. Desired changes don't just come about by themselves; we must act to produce them. Such a statement may seem a little obvious — all first principles generally are — but it brings home a fact of life: you can't change while you remain in a state of inertia. If you're going to break the habit of being poor — and it's only a habit — you will have to exert a force to do it. It won't happen without it.

> No change takes place unless a force is applied.

So the first law of human change is: *Do something.*

Let's continue with Physics 101. Newton's second law states that the bigger something is, the harder it is to move. In scientific language, the acceleration an object experiences multiplied by the mass of that object is equal to the net force acting upon it; that is, Force = Mass x Acceleration. So if a force of the same magnitude acts on two objects of different mass, the object with the larger mass will have a lower acceleration.

> The greater the mountain you have to move, the more dynamite you need.

The same is true of personal change. The greater the problem, the greater the force needed to produce the same change. If you've been stuck in a rut for 10 years, and the Bitch Matrix has become very much part of you, a greater force is needed to change your life than if you're just having a couple of bad years. People make this mistake all the time, when trying to change themselves. Someone who has spent the last 30 years making ends meet is going to have to do a lot more work to change behaviour and thought patterns than someone who has just left school and started to make a living.

Although it also appears obvious, a lot of people don't realise that the amount of energy they must exert to bring about a desired behavioural change is in direct proportion to the size of their problem.

The second law of human change is therefore: *Do the right something.*

Newton's third law is also very straightforward: to every force there is an equal and opposite reaction. The recoil of a gun when it's fired best illustrates this. This fundamental principle, which later

> Do something that's the opposite of what you've been doing.

developed into the law of conservation of momentum, can also be applied to human change. It explains why the body reacts to change or why depression can often accompany an altered behaviour pattern. The body reacts to the denial of whatever pleasure it received from earlier behaviour; that is, it exerts a reactionary force equal and opposite to the force of change.

Newton's third law explains why changing behaviour is often construed as a battle. There are always forces working against what we're trying to achieve. But if we increase the forces working to change the behaviour (motivation, therapy, goal-setting, etc),

> Habit builds resistance to change.

we create a net force (that is, the sum of the two opposite forces) greater than zero, and then change will happen.

The third law of human change is therefore: *Do something that is the opposite of what you've been doing.*

This simple formula has been an incredibly powerful tool for people I know who have created real change in their lives. It's based on the observation that habit builds resistance to change. In order to break down that resistance, you have to fight force of habit with the force of a new habit.

Aristotle understood this. He said that we are not what we do, but what we *repeatedly* do.

Bad money habits, built up over years, resist change as much as if you've been hooked on an addictive substance. It is no exaggeration to say that all the big addictions of life — smoking, alcohol, sugar, sex, gambling, drugs — only differ from the other bad habits we pick up in the severity of their consequences. They are all habits, and thus give us short-term pleasure.

Compulsive spending is a good example. Grace, as we mentioned before, knew that to break the habit of her weekly binge — of rewarding herself for a week of work — she had to step into the Choice Gap and make a choice. But that was not enough. If she followed Newton's laws, she would have to have the same passion with which she spent her money, and do something that was the opposite of what she had been doing. She had to find out the average amount she spent on her impulsive indulgence, and then *actively* save that as soon as her salary cheque was in her hand. She had to counteract one force of habit with another force of habit.

Another surprise from the class was Phil. He was so quiet most of the time that I sometimes found myself wanting to scream at him, just to see if he was still breathing. Unlike the others, his face showed little, so I had no idea how he was taking any of this.

He rang me during the week and asked to see me. I thought he had taken my call to commitment seriously and, being unable to articulate what he truly wanted in life, had decided to pull out. I was, happily, wrong.

Phil was a taxi driver. He also had two degrees, spoke a couple of languages and had dabbled in more careers than most of us would have in six lifetimes. He was in his mid-thirties, had never married, and had taken up doing the odd shift in a taxi just to get by. The conversation in my apartment that Thursday night changed direction when he reached into his knapsack and pulled out what looked like a thousand pages of typed manuscript.

'You write?' I asked.

'Badly,' he answered.

'How do you know it's bad? Has someone told you?'

'Not really. I do a lot of reading and I just know — instinctively — what bad writing is.'

He handed me some sheets of paper selected from the stack he was having trouble keeping together.

'I have started nine novels in the last three years, and not a single one of them has been finished.'

It would have been very foolish of me to fire off a one-size-fits-all solution and suggest that Phil drop everything he's doing and concentrate full-time on his writing. I had no idea whether what he wrote was any good, or whether it had any commercial value.

It was not his writing I was interested in, but the underlying patterns of behaviour. As he talked I identified a recurrent theme: Phil had a habit of not finishing things, and lately it had worsened. In his own words, he was constantly looking for ways to distract himself. He told me the exercise we had done in class of stepping forward unchanged into the future — the Bridget Jones Exercise — had affected him quite deeply, and he was petrified that if he continued to do what he was doing (Newton's first law), he would have very little ahead of him.

I had to work quickly to establish a common register of communication, because Phil and I were very different. Phil was an intellectual and I was not. Phil had no head for business and I did. What gave him his greatest thrills were things like a great art-house film, an absorbing historical biography or a classical music concert. He even went to poetry readings. In other words, what he was *really, really* interested in would, it seemed, not create wealth measured in monetary terms, unless he was particularly talented and could find a way of marketing that talent. So I dived in head-first with my questions.

'Do you know what you *really, really* want in life?'

'Yes. I want to not work.'

I was not surprised. I have met many people, like Phil, who find any use of their time that is not directly connected to nourishing their minds or interests somehow a burden. They are not interested in career success or in developing their own marketability. Not even the idea of being CEO of a large multinational, or a Wall Street wizard, or even a bestselling author, attracts them. They simply want enough time and financial resources so that they can fill their world with what truly interests them.

There's a lot to be said for people like Phil. They are usually genuine thinkers, interesting conversation partners, and make special contributions to society. A society without philosophers, writers, artists and intellectuals — even if they never make it to market — would indeed be a truly impoverished one. The problem is, of course, that while there's something to be said for being a person of leisure and culture, someone has to pay the bills.

At the heart of Phil's problem was an indifference to money. He saw it as a means to an end, like most of us, and was not interested in putting in the effort to make it any more important than that.

'Would you do anything and everything not to have to work for a living — I mean by your definition of work?'

Phil didn't answer. His mind must have been tossing around the things we had discussed so far: zero-option commitment, the unbreakable promise.

'By that, I mean everything,' I continued. 'You won't do anything unrelated to this one single goal until you have reached it. Can you become totally and unconditionally obsessed until you have achieved your goal of being free from work?'

'No more new interests? No more reading or concerts?

'Nah. Not unless they're related to this goal.'

'But you have to relax at some time, don't you?'

'Sounds to me as if that's all you've been doing,' I said with a slight laugh. 'And anyway, you can start to relax after you've actually done something.'

As it turned out, Phil had a brilliant idea for how to make money. He also admitted that within two years it could be up and running and generating income.

'But I've always had big ideas. The problem is ... '

'You never actually do anything about them,' I interrupted. 'Newton's first law.' I briefly explained the three laws of personal change that would be the subject of the coming session.

'Well I start, but then something happens. I usually go on to something else.'

'That generally means you're not applying enough force to get underway. Newton's second law. And you're not doing the opposite of letting yourself be distracted. Newton's third law.'

Phil left with plenty to think about. He went home with the task of focusing on the small things. The big picture will be different, I told him, if its basic units of composition are different. His task was to focus on the elements of his day. What could he do in the opposite direction that would move him towards his goal? It was an easy method — just do the opposite of what is not productive. I had no doubt he had the creativity to come up with a radical plan of action.

The only disappointment of the week was Leon. He telephoned to tell me that he didn't really think he was ready to go as far as I was suggesting. He couldn't in all honesty clarify what he truly wanted in life. I appreciated his honesty, and told him that if he pretended, or came up with something to which he was only half-committed, he would fail anyway.

When the remaining six arrived for this session, there was excitement in the air. They started to swap stories about the time they had put into clarifying what they *really, really* wanted in life. One by one I took their postcards, without looking at them.

'Aren't you going to read them?' Cathy asked.

'Nope,' I said. 'If you wrote them for me, they're worthless.'

Nothing like a strong statement to get the show rolling.

After I had explained Newton's three laws of human change to them, I asked if they knew why I turned to physics to explain behaviour. Why had I moved away from psychology to explain human behaviour?

'Because it's harder to make up a story in physics,' Margaret said. She was, as always, right on the mark.

'That's it. You've heard me talk to you about the importance of getting the facts right; separating reality from your interpretation of it. And here,' I said, 'are all the messages of our time together summed up in one truth. Being rich or poor is about'... and I turned to the whiteboard and wrote:

CAUSE AND EFFECT.

'Now here comes my radical bit of free thinking,' I said. 'I want you all to stop thinking about the reasons for your behaviour. You could fill books with fascinating reasons, spend years coming up with them, delving into your past, analysing long-held beliefs.

That's all good, but as I said right from day one, if you do this, you won't have cleared the water, you will have just stirred up more of the mud.

'Don't think "reasons" for your actions; think "causes".' I took a ball out of my gym bag and tossed it towards Andy. He caught it.

'What does it matter if I had a perfectly good or a perfectly wicked reason for throwing that ball at Andy? The point is that the position of the ball has now changed because I exerted a force on it. The ball doesn't care why I did it. It's just in a different place. The cause was my throwing and the effect is that it is now in a different location. Oh, I could tell you lots of stories. I could make you laugh or weep, get you angry with me or get you to sympathise with me. But so what? The ball's location has changed because I threw it. Cause and effect.

'I don't know about you, but I find human behaviour so complicated that the more I look at it, the more confused I am. Of course the complex processes in our minds make us fascinating individuals, but I think that if we could just place less emphasis on the million theories about *why* we act in certain ways and instead start to focus on *what* we do, we could see a way out of the mess.

'As superficial and clinical as it sounds, I am daring you to treat your behaviour as simple cause and effect relations. You have nothing in the bank because either you didn't put it in there or you took it out. Don't give me the dramas. Treat it like a business; your financial position is no more than the difference between money in and money out.'

I wrote on the board:

MONEY IN. MONEY OUT.

'So, tell me why are you not rich.'

'Because we've done nothing about it,' Mitch said.

'Exactly. You go nowhere, or continue to behave in exactly the same way, unless you apply a net force to change the situation. Obvious? Someone was sure to have said that about Newton's work. But I will bet anything that once you apply the initial effort, once that ball stops going in the same direction with a constant velocity, you'll be saying to yourself, "It's so obvious. Why didn't I realise it before?"'

'Toney, were you a science major?' Cathy suddenly asked.

'No. I probably know less about science than anyone here. But I love the way science works — it sticks to the facts. Similarly, businesses succeed, wealth creation plans work, investment strategies bear fruit, when they're based on facts — market statistics, capital return, cash flow management, etc. Of course businesses can also be inspiring and exciting – they can make great stories — but no amount of inspiration will make a business work unless it eventually shows up as cold, boring, black and white numbers on a balance sheet. Human change — your change — must also be based on facts.'

'Toney, there's something missing from this view. Mitch knows he has to do something, but somehow can't,' Mitch said.

'Can't? Of course Mitch can't if he hasn't got the potential to do it. Back to physics. When a force operates, it changes potential energy into the kinetic energy of movement. So Mitch is right. Without potential energy you can't create a force. So the real problem is that Mitch doesn't believe he has the potential to change.'

The reason why so little is done is because so little is attempted.

'Look,' I added, 'the very idea that we can change ourselves is a relatively recent idea. For thousands of years, the nature of individuals, their "personality caste", even the purpose of their lives, were believed to be as permanent as the colour of their skin. We used to believe that every human frailty and spark of genius was a manufacturing decision of God, and that a human being could not attempt change without somehow interfering in this divine plan. We were stuck with it. We believed that we didn't have the potential energy — the power needed to create a force that would bring about change. However, with the founding of the New World, a few centuries of religious reform, and the rise of the new sciences, "free will" — the capacity to choose one's behaviour — was eventually reinstated. We realised that we can change anything that it is possible to change because we have the potential to change to it.'

'But what happened to the idea of accepting yourself? Won't it cause frustration to try to change what can't be changed?' Margaret asked.

> You can only change what can reasonably be changed.

'Yes, but apart from the obvious, it is difficult to find anything that can't be changed. How much you change depends entirely on the force you apply to bring about that change. How far this ball moves will depend on the force you exert on it. If you want it to go as far as the moon, you will need to launch it on the back of a rocket. If you want to throw it out the window, you will need a certain amount of force to do that. Either way, it will stay right here in front of me until you do something.

'We used to think accepting ourselves was the right thing to do. And accepting those things we can't change — there are very few — is of course sensible. Accepting absolutely everything about ourselves, however, is a cop-out. Let's go a step further and say that to accept yourself unconditionally is

> Who said self-acceptance is a virtue? It could also be a cop-out.

about the worst thing you can do. Now we're really beginning to think radically.

'A fundamental principle of powerful personal change is that you don't have to accept your life, because your life can always be better than, and different from, the one you're living at present. You can always reinvent yourself, move towards the "meta-you". Your life can be as different from one moment to the next as you want, if the demands you make on yourself are reasonable. Given the diversity of people's life circumstances, that may sound oversimplified, but in the context of an individual making a rational claim on life, it's the first law of self-fulfilment. It might require a lot of courage, as you live through inevitable disappointment and frustration, but what's the alternative? A sort of "This is my lot in life — it's not a lot, but it's my life" attitude? Do you really want the finality of retirement at entry-level?

'Think of the horror of a half-lived life. Do you really want to go through the next 20, 30, 40 years of life without discernible growth? Isn't it much more exciting to know that your life can be whatever you reasonably want it to be? That is the trouble with the Bitch Matrix. Someone told you to accept yourself; that there was nothing you could do about it. You've been living with this idea for so long that you believe change is not possible. But change, radical and permanent change, is possible.

'No one is suggesting you go over the top. If you don't have a pair of wings, the chances are that no matter how much you believe you can fly, you're probably better off reserving a flight on a normal commercial airliner for transcontinental travel. Some things are as impossible as square circles. Quitting the Bitch Matrix for good, however, is definitely not a square circle.

> A half-lived life is always a half-wanted one.

'If you're not yet convinced that you can be empowered to bring about this radical self-actualisation, try the following: imagine someone was threatening to slice your mother up in front of you, or chop off your son's right leg, if you didn't change. Would you still insist that you couldn't change? Of course you wouldn't, because in such serious situations, power comes to us all. If you made making money and gaining financial freedom as serious as that, if you convinced yourself they had the finality of a life-threatening choice, do you think you would fail at them? Of course not.'

'So what are you all waiting for? You have the potential to change, so do something, do the right something, and make sure it's the opposite of what hasn't been going right.

'Next week, we're going to look at what those right somethings are.'

9. The rulebook of the rich: Part 1

I was struggling to keep the focus of the course on making money. It had become clear to everyone that what they were learning could be used to bring about real changes in their whole lives, not just their finances. I resisted the temptation as much as I could because growing rich is an excellent teaching vehicle for separating facts from the little personal fictions we build around those facts, because how much money you have is a measurable fact.

It was also clear to me that some of the group were already thinking beyond the money context, but I had to try to keep wealth creation as our main reference, otherwise we could easily get diverted by the other exciting ramifications of what we were learning.

> Universal rules are followed by necessity; personal rules by choice.

In wealth creation, there are universal rules and there are personal rules. In this part of the journey, we are going to look at both kinds as we prepare for the serious task of writing our own rulebooks.

We have already talked about the law of cause and effect and Newton's laws of motion. These are just two of the many universal, unchangeable rules of nature which we have no choice but to obey. This sort of rule is neither good nor bad, and it operates regardless of what you think about it. Similarly, many of the rules governing wealth creation have nothing to do with your opinion of them: they are fixed rules that have worked for centuries, and they have very little to do with an individual's ability, attitude or circumstances.

Personal rules, on the other hand, work for some people and not for others, and work at certain times and not at others. These rules depend very much on circumstances, and on an individual's personality and belief systems.

We all have rulebooks, whether we have consciously created them or not. In fact, we have thousands of behavioural rules which govern our relationships with ourselves and with others. Most people can probably get through life quite well without being aware of their own personal set of social behaviour rules. But we can't do that with our personal set of financial behaviour rules. Working out these rules is not only a very important step in the growth of financial intelligence; it's also a lot of fun.

When I embarked on a personal growth program of promise-keeping, I encountered a very straightforward problem: what rules of behaviour did I need in order to keep the promises I had made to myself? If I were to promise myself, for example, that I would work unstintingly towards a financial goal, I needed rules that

> Writing a personal rulebook keeps you accountable for the promises you make.

would keep me focused on that goal and call me to account. It was then that I started looking at the rules the rich play by and making some of them my own.

So I began to write my own rulebook. I soon found that this was an excellent way to clarify what were the really important governing principles of my life. It was also a way of introducing a measure of discipline into my life. I think about these rules all the time. I take them very seriously. I don't make rules that I can't keep and I don't make silly rules. I make only rules that reflect my values and make my life more productive and purposeful.

> A rulebook brings structured discipline to your life.

One of the most striking attributes of the rich when it comes to rule-making is their pragmatism. To successful people, a worthwhile rule is simply one that works. How interesting or original the rule is doesn't really matter.

> Good rules are simple, memorable and rewarding.

If you complicate a rule it will lose its power. If you make it long-winded you'll probably never remember it, and if it doesn't carry its own reward, it will be as pointless as discipline for its own sake.

During this session I presented some of the best-known rules of the Rich Matrix — the common beliefs of the rich. One by one we explored the theory behind them and examined practical ways to apply them.

I told everyone in the group to buy a very special book. It was important that it wasn't just any old cheap notebook, because they would be treating this book with near reverence, and carrying it with them for life. This would be their private rulebook, where the rules they choose to live by and the promises they make would be recorded.

In view of the seriousness of what they are going to write in their rulebook, it is also very important that they take their time and be very sure about what they are committing to before they write anything in the book. There can be no changing their mind, no 'buts' or qualifications. A rule is an expression of zero-option empowerment, and as such, it will be something they will blindly, unequivocally and passionately adhere to. Not living by any of these rules, or breaking any of the promises, is self-betrayal. Keeping them, being true to one's word, on the other hand, is evidence of the triumph of the self.

The format is simple: first the rule, then the promises which relate to the rule. Each rule can have any number of promises, but a new promise can only be added once the previous promise has either been kept or become automatic behaviour, and that can take weeks, months, even years.

Some people tell me that this is mad, obsessive and impossible. 'You are setting people up for disappointment,' they say. Perhaps they are right. But I have read all the books in the bookshop, gone to all the seminars on the circuit ... and yet stayed at the starting line. I didn't move off that line until I took a principle, learned it, and applied it in my life unconditionally.

Rule-making and promise-keeping was my way out of the Bridget Jones Syndrome, and it had to be done with absolute commitment.

After everyone had arrived and settled down I turned to the first slide and launched straight into the rules of the game.

Rule 1: You control your life by controlling your time.

'We've established that being in the Rich Matrix is about being in control of your life. Until you take control of your life, the only other way wealth can come into your life is by pure accident, and the odds of that happening are not very encouraging. One of the most important aspects of your life, something over which you must exercise total — even dictatorial — control, is time.

'We all exist in time. It defines whether we are at the beginning, the middle or the end of our lives. There is no life, as far as we know, which does not exist in time. It makes very good sense, therefore, to believe that controlling our lives and controlling our time go hand in hand.'

I looked around the room for my first victim.

'Andy, how old is Andy?'

'Andy is 28.'

'Is that 28 exactly, to the very day?

'No. It's 28 and seven months.'

'To the very day?'

'No,' he said, and thought briefly. 'Actually, 28 years and seven months and 18 days.'

'Does Andy realise that those seven months and 18 days are important? That he can't just forget about them like that?'

Andy signalled his understanding with a vigorous nod.

'Does Andy have any idea how much Bill Gates makes in seven months and 18 days? Don't answer that, because neither do I, but I think we all get my point. If you made as much money as Gates in a day, would seven months and 18 days be written off just like that?

'Or consider this. What would Margaret do if she knew she had only 10,000 litres of water for her life and not a drop more?'

'She'd make sure it lasted a lifetime. She'd probably ration it. Keep a record of how she's using it. Share it very sparingly.' She turned to Mitch and laughed, 'Sorry, honey, get your own.'

'OK. Now let's say Margaret lives until she is 80. Not a minute longer. Would she do the same with her time?'

Margaret smiled. She had got the point.

Time, unlike water, is a non-renewable resource.

'Imagine that you were allocated only a certain amount of sunlight or water in your life. If you knew that there would be no more than that for you, ever, would you waste any of it? One of the first things you'd want to know is how to use it wisely. It's the same with time, which, unlike natural resources, is non-renewable. Regardless of what you do with your life or what grandiose schemes you have in mind, there are only a certain number of seconds in a day (86,400, actually), days in a year and years in your lifetime. For us mortals, time is not infinite; we are allotted a certain number of minutes. No more, no less. Time is, I repeat, a *non-renewable* resource. Because it is non-renewable, it is, in a sense, even more valuable than sunlight or water.

'Here's another example. What was Grace doing last Friday night at 7.00pm?'

'Watching TV probably.'

'What was on?'

'Grace can't remember.'

'Grace can't remember because she was passing her time by doing something which wasn't important enough to remember. Grace may have spent two hours or more doing whatever it was that was not important.'

'C'mon, Toney,' Margaret interrupted. 'I'm not going to clock my every waking moment. You'll turn me into a neurotic.'

'I'm not asking us to. I'm asking us to become aware of how we disrespect time. It's our most valuable resource and we don't even respect it enough to acknowledge it. We even feel no guilt when we say we are "just killing time".

You will never control your time unless you give it absolute importance.

'Because your life is so bound up in time, you will never control it unless you control your time, and you will never control your time until you give it the importance owed to it. If you don't take control of your time, forget any hope of wealth creation; it takes time and needs time — some of the limited, valuable time allotted to you.

'So who can suggest some rules or promises they might make regarding time? Remember, we're not going to put these into our rulebooks yet. We're only considering them for the moment. Commitment to a rule or a promise is very serious.'

Phil raised his hand again. *Why is he still doing that?* I thought.

'Phil is going to spend a whole week thinking about the importance of time.'

'Does Phil realise what that means? Can Phil really commit a week of his life to focus, almost exclusively, on the priority of time in his life?'

Phil didn't answer, absorbed in his own thoughts.

'And Andy is going to enrol in a course on time management,' said Andy.

> Because time is so precious, time management is one of the most useful subjects you can study.

'Great. That's specific. That's achievable. It's something you can promise to do and then actually do. There are hundreds of good ideas and courses around. I have been known to tell people that a time management course could be the most important course they ever do, because it is the beginning of greater productivity, and therefore a useful tool for a fully lived life. The sooner you start to control your time, the sooner you will be making choices that lead to greater wealth.'

'Cathy is going to buy an organiser and seriously get into the habit of having it on her at all times.'

'If Cathy turns that into a promise, that is a big commitment. It means that it will be one of the first things to greet her in the morning. She will have to keep it with her mobile phone or with something she knows she will take with her. It will also be one of the last things she says "good night" to. It will have to be part of her day, as compulsory as clothes. Does Cathy understand that? Does Cathy understand that she will have to be obsessed by her organiser, at least during the conscious competence stage? I mean really fanatical about it. Otherwise, it'll just be a short-lived experiment.'

'I know,' said Margaret. 'I think a good rule of practice would be that every time Margaret says she doesn't have time to do something, she will instead say that she is more interested in doing something else.'

> Don't say you don't have time; say you are more interested in doing something else.

'I like that. Another rule used by a friend of mine is to say "no" to a time-robber at least once a day. She deliberately looks for activities that are a waste of time, or people who rob her of her time, and says "no" to one at least once a day. She told me that she has kept this simple rule for over a year, and it is now a daily habit. She also said that it had made her aware of the almost endless supply of time-robbing activities in her life, the hundreds of distractions. If this is the only rule or promise she keeps throughout her life, it will have made a huge difference.

'Let's move onto rule number two,' I said.

Rule 2: Time is not money, but you should act as if it is.

'I don't know who came up with the equation that time is money, but it's wrong. Time is not money. Unlike time, money is a renewable resource — you can always get more. Time, as I have said, is non-renewable, non-negotiable and non-refundable. It is more valuable than any amount of money. Ask the billionaire on an early deathbed which is more important. Would she want another billion or another 10 years?

'So if, for example, someone went on the internet and moved all Cathy's funds from her bank account into theirs, how would she feel?'

'She'd be as pissed as all hell,' Cathy said, sounding surprised that I had used her as an example.

'Why, then, isn't Cathy furious — more than furious, why isn't she absolutely outraged — when someone steals her time? She should be fuming, because there's no way of getting stolen time back. Like money, time can be stolen from you, but it cannot be returned by those who stole it or by any kind of victims' compensation fund. Once stolen, it's gone for good.

'The rich have a practical solution, as always. Time might not be the same as money, but it is useful to think of it as if it is. Think about billing an imaginary someone for every hour of the day, putting a price tag on every minute of your day.'

'Bullshit,' Margaret almost leaped to her feet. 'Pardon my language, but some activities, such as time with my — sorry, Margaret's — husband, do not carry a price tag. When we make love we're not going to bill each other for our time. Some things are priceless.'

'Phil agrees,' Phil said. 'You can't put a price to an hour spent watching the sunrise. You would kill all the poetry of life.'

'That's nonsense, both of you. This is not a course about the finer things of life. This is a course about money. I never promised to increase your appreciation of sunrises or deepen your love life. I promised to set you on the road to wealth — our destination is a black and white balance sheet. Thinking in terms of billable hours is not going to make you boring or machine-like; it's

> Think of your day as 24 billable hours. Your eyes will be opened to your earning potential.

going to make you more realistic about your earning potential. I love to watch the sunrise and make love as much as the rest of you, but neither is going to add to my balance sheet. Get over it, all of you.'

There was silence. To this day, I will never forget the look of incredulity on their faces.

'Every minute carries a price tag. Naturally, for some activities we are more than willing to pay the price. Furthermore, when you know that the time you spend with someone you love carries a price tag, you are more likely to put more into it and get more out of it.'

'Cathy has no idea how she's going to live like this,' Cathy said. 'It sounds so awful.'

'Why is it awful? Time killed, enjoyed, hated or billed is just time spent. There's nothing nice or awful about it. It's time gone. That's all. You must suspend your emotions if you are going to get to the essence of time. And I have an exercise that is really going to make you look at the fact of time the same way you look at a calculator.

'First, just take an ordinary day out of your life and try to bill every hour of that day at an hourly rate. It's a weird and obsessive way of looking at things — and you'd go mad if you did it all the time — but for one day it's worth trying. It is, after all, what lawyers do.'

'Tell me about it,' Mitch said. There was obviously a story there, but I moved on.

'Let's say you bill yourself out at $50 an hour. Assuming you work eight hours a day, you are owed $400. You sleep eight hours and another eight hours are accounted for by all the normal things in a person's life — eating, relaxing, spending time with the family, etc. Now we move to the second part of the exercise. Let's say we found that we could retrieve one hour 20 minutes a day by cutting out procrastination, unnecessary meetings, passive TV, pottering around, etc. In a six day week you would save eight hours — in other words, your weekly income would theoretically increase by $400, from $2000 to $2400; a whopping 20 per cent increase. This assumes, of course, that the time you retrieve is spent making money — either immediately payable or payable in the future.'

I paused to let it sink in.

'Of course, no one will ever be happy thinking about life in terms of billable hours. The point of the exercise is that it can help you add value to time, and therefore trigger your rich-thinking mode. So, any suggestions on this rule?'

> Stop time from flowing down the time drain.

Margaret spoke again. 'OK. Margaret will give it a go. Since she is addicted to sitting in coffee shops, she might make it a rule to mentally add her hourly rate to the coffee bill. Over two hours, two cups of coffee at $2.50 each would in fact cost $105.'

'Not to mention how much income lots of those saved $100s could have made,' I added.

Rule 3: You control your life by controlling your space.

'The next rule is about space. The two most important co-ordinates of the material world are time and space; they define our world. Like time, your space is finite. You only have a certain amount of space in your life, and we are now going to look at the importance of controlling that space.

'When I say "space", I don't just mean the physical space of your living room or office. I am also referring to your personal space.

'Controlling space is as important as controlling time. The best way to increase space in your life is to start simplifying your life.

'Putting the space you have into order is part of learning to focus on what is really important; it's the prelude to being able to concentrate on improving your financial situation. I noticed that when I started on an anti-clutter campaign — not just the thousands of useless things in my life, but also the clutter of thoughts, people, undirected emotions, wild hopes ... the whole lot — I began to see the relationship between space and wealth.

A chaotic financial life is often reflected in a chaotic personal space.

'I realised that my life was messy. My past was unordered, my present was chaotic, and my future would probably be the same. So I started with my physical space, decided to sweep out everything that was clutter and assigned specific places to what remained. Everything would have its particular space — which of course is subtracted from the total, finite space of my life.

'It was an enormous task, and I was impossible to live with at the time. I kept looking at things and wondering why the hell I had them. So I marked for extinction everything that served absolutely no purpose in my life.

Get rid of everything that serves no purpose.

'I recommend this tactic for anyone moving house, because I managed to reduce my world to a few boxes of really valuable items. The rest was sent to a charity shop. And guess what? It hurt. But you cannot imagine how liberating it was. I felt that I could breathe again.

'Then I started on my computer files. I managed to get all my computer files onto four CDs. The rest I annihilated, with a few clicks of the mouse. Next were my wardrobe, my car and my office. Does anyone know where all this is leading?'

No answer.

The more manageable your physical space is, the more manageable your mental space will be.

'I was making my life more physically manageable, and as a result, it was becoming more mentally manageable. I actually started to think more clearly, and my stress levels plummeted. Don't ask me why this is so, but others will tell you the same thing. I suppose it has something to do with outer reality being a reflection of inner reality. I don't really care about the reason. It just worked. Like magic, I tell you, like magic.'

'What's this got to do with making money?' Mitch asked. 'I can't see how having an ordered garage is going to affect that balance sheet you keep talking about.'

'It has a knock-on effect. When I became committed to simplifying my life, I began to see everything more clearly, and soon I also began to see what was actually happening to my money. I had bank accounts that were serving no purpose, credit cards I never used, telephone services I was paying for but that I had forgotten about. I had business plans that I had written off but that still haunted me, thus taking up valuable space in my head. I even found a stack of shares I had forgotten about. All of these were taking up my mental and physical space.'

> Don't waste valuable space in your head.

'That makes sense to Andy. The fewer things that distract you, the easier it is to keep your concentration.'

'Pretty simple, isn't it? But what a powerful principle!'

'Cathy would find it hard to throw away things. She's still got clothes with the price tag on them, but it would break her heart to see them go.'

'I am going to throw out a challenge to Cathy. If she is serious about taking control of her life, then she has to be serious about freeing up her own space. Cathy should dare herself to try. And really trash it. Don't put it all the attic.' I said smiling. 'That's cheating.'

Cathy was not looking happy.

'I said it hurts, Cathy. And it does. But the payback is

almost unbelievable. Anyway, think about it and let's move on to another of my favourite rules.'

Rule 4: Brand yourself.

'Stories about the power of positive thinking have been around a long time,' I started.

'Yes. And Margaret is getting really negative about hearing it again,' Margaret said jokingly.

'But the rule works: negative beliefs are self-defeating and positive beliefs are self-sustaining. However, I am going to go a little further with positive thinking, because I agree with Margaret. Babbling inane positive affirmations about yourself is just hocus-pocus. It makes more business sense — and remember, that's why we're here — to instead think of yourself as a brand.

'Would you want yourself to be a cheap and nasty brand or a high-quality brand? Would you want to say positive or negative things about your brand? You don't have to be a marketing wizard to know that the difference between one brand and other is very often only a matter of image — of what is thought about the brand and what is said about it. So many top brands are no different from their poorer relatives except in how they are perceived. You also don't have to be a genius to work out that the poor go for cheaper brands, not only because of lack of money, but because that's where they pitch themselves.'

> Think of yourself as a brand in need of a good marketing plan.

'I don't get it, ' Mitch said.

'Mitch likes cars, right?'

'He sure does. He hopes to get a new one next year.'

'Top of the range, luxury car, I suppose?'

'No. He will never be able to afford anything more than a second-hand car.'

'Of course. No one could possibly imagine such a cheap product like Mitch behind a classy car,' I said sarcastically.

The class laughed. The point was very obvious.

'With that sort of thinking, Mitch will only ever get rich by accident. What we have been doing over the last few months is learning how not to live by accident. If that's how you think you will grow rich, you may as well wait around until your lottery numbers come up. No, you don't get rich by accident, in the same way as you don't create a great brand by accident.

> Few brands succeed by accident, neither will you.

'You make money by proclaiming yourself a top brand worth top dollars. Of course you're no better than the next person, but that won't stop you being perceived as better.'

'Margaret thinks that sounds corny,' Margaret said.

'It is corny. But does that mean it's not true?' I asked. 'Margaret, how much does Margaret think she could earn in a year?'

'Not much. She hasn't found any money-making idea yet.'

> Brand yourself as ordinary and you'll carry the corresponding price tag.

'But the idea she will find one — and she will find one — is already limited by her "not much" thinking. Her idea is already doomed to make "not much"; any extra will be an accident. She has already branded herself as ordinary. Margaret won't earn much because according to her own brand statements, her brand value isn't worth much.

'Does anyone have any practical suggestions about how we might go about increasing our own brand value?'

As I expected, the question was greeted with a room full of blank stares.

'I have one. Treat yourselves like a business and brand yourselves. Margaret Inc. Mitch Pty Ltd. Cathy Enterprises. Phil Holdings. The Grace Company. Andy Investments.'

'We'll merge,' Margaret said, smiling and looking at Mitch. 'M&M Pty Ltd.'

'Now, apart from hard work, what really makes a company? What will attract someone to Cathy Enterprises?'

'A good deal,' Cathy said.

'So when you buy a bottle of Coke, you think to yourself, *This cost so much to make and I am only paying this much for it? Wow! That's a great deal!*'

'No of course not.'

'Coca-Cola is 90 per cent image. Its brand equity is worth far more than all its physical assets combined. It sells because it looks good and Coca-Cola makes statements about how good it is.

> You must look good and sound good to add value to your personal brand.

Similarly, you must look good and sound good to add value to your brand.'

'So Grace can go out and buy really expensive clothes and expect that somehow they'll be paid for?'

'Grace might be able to. But for Grace Inc., new clothes would only be purchased if they go to the primary goal of business — to make money. You see, when you think of yourself as a business, you can apply business principles to every part of your life. Businesses which succeed do so on

> Apply the principles of good business management to life management.

the basis of a budget, a sales forecast, planned growth, the right strategies and, of course, the killer brand.'

'That makes sense to Phil. When you brand, you focus on what makes your product different. That's what you sell.'

'Exactly.' Phil must have seen the next slide.

Rule 5: Find your USP (Unique Selling Proposition).

'You brand what you are going to sell, and what you are going to sell is what makes you different. Remember how we talked about authenticity — about finding the one attribute or talent that defined you? Well, that's the branded you; it's what you do best; it's the business of the real you. If a company were excellent at making widgets — and it made the best on the market — would it turn to making pizzas? Of course not. A successful company focuses on what it does best and builds its brand on that. This is exactly what you need to do.

'What is your USP? If you think there is none, there's the door. Sorry you've wasted your time. No company will survive without something to sell and neither will you without something to sell. And everyone has something about themselves that is marketable. Everyone.

'Finding your USP is probably not going to happen tonight. But it's a serious search; it's related to what you want out of life — what you've written on those postcards. If what you want out of life cannot be achieved through the talent or skill that defines you — your USP — it's never going to happen.

> Your USP is what you do best.

'Now I don't want you to tell me what your USP is, not yet, but can you suggest how you might go about finding it, if you don't already know?'

'What about taking a personality test to find our strengths?' Cathy asked.

'That's not a bad idea. The Myers-Briggs test, which determines how you process information, is a good personality assessment tool. It helps you decide which jobs you would be good at and which you probably wouldn't do well at. But I think it's more rewarding just to look at yourself. I said it right at the beginning of the course: you know yourself. You know, instinctively, who you are. You know yourself better than anyone else knows you. So you know what your USP because it's what you do best and what you love doing.'

'I believe that the way to get a thing done is to set a delivery time, so now we are going to set a date to define your USP. If you don't find it by that date, give up. You're doomed to having no money.'

> Set a deadline for finding your USP.

'How rude!' Grace said with a laugh.

'I'm deadly serious, Grace. It's not just a fanciful idea to go floating off into space. Finding your USP is a deliverable. Deliver it or quit.'

I reached into my bag of tricks and brought out a calendar. 'Surprise. This is to show you just how serious you have to be about delivering. I am going to pass this around the class. You can take your time, but I want you to circle your deadline date and write your name next to it. I will ring you on that day. You'd better have found your USP, or it's the last time we'll speak together.' I pulled the most serious face possible. 'I mean it.'

You could have heard the proverbial pin drop.

'Remember the either/or position, everyone? Well, it's one of those situations now. Set a delivery date or you'll be wandering around the periphery for years to come. You'll stay a peripheroid. Find your talent. Find what is going to be at the basis of making lots of money ... or quit.'

> If you don't set a delivery time for your USP, you'll stay a peripheroid.

I knew these next few sessions were going to be tough and I was beginning to feel drained, but I was determined that the course would bring about a real change in thinking and behaving. If I had to serve it to them cold, so be it. Their thinking must be changed; really, measurably, permanently changed.

So I soldiered on, without any apology.

Rule 6: Do something once and sell it many times.

'When you find the one thing you do really well, the one thing that makes you feel authentic, you need to sell it. Not once, but many times.

'Unless you're exceptionally fortunate, you will never grow rich by doing something once and selling it only once. Or course this is exactly what most of the world's workforce does. We go to work, sell our time, and then come back the next day and sell our time again.

'But, you will say, this is the way the world works; there are jobs that have to be done which are neither inspirational nor lucrative and someone has to do them. True, and I would add, there are lots of people who are quite happy doing them. In fact, I can remember times in my life when I had jobs that could barely pay the rent, yet I was happy, simply because I felt useful and the work I was doing had a purpose — for one thing, it paid the rent! But we're not talking here about a personal sense of worth; we're talking about a definite way to grow financial worth — do something once and sell it many times. Of course, it's not possible for everyone to do that, but, if you can do it, it's a sure way to make money.'

'An even better rule is to do something once and get others to sell it many times. That's how franchising works, and in private business it's close to nirvana. It is also the operational principle behind personal investing. When you are investing your money, you are actually selling it. You made it once and you keep on selling it. That's why you can grow rich on wise investment. That's why people grow rich on property. They put the effort into getting the first investment property, and the rest is really selling that same first effort. As they invest more and more from the proceeds of previous investments, they are in fact

> An even better rule is to do something once and get others to sell it many times.

selling the same thing. They are not working to earn more; they are just selling more.

'So when you're looking for the one idea that will make you money, look for the one that you only have to do once. If Phil puts his effort into actually getting a book published, for example, he doesn't have to rewrite it. He just has to sell it over and over again. That's an easy example. What about Cathy?'

'Cathy might start her own restaurant.'

'And if Cathy is still doing all the work in that restaurant after, say, three years, would Cathy's restaurant be making her rich?'

'Probably not.'

'Right. Rich people make sure their original effort is soon not required, which frees them up to create something else that will sell itself many times. While you keep putting in the same effort for the same one-off return you will remain forever enslaved in the salary trap. You will remain a labourer. A slave building someone else's pyramid.'

I spiced it up by behaving like an Egyptian slave dragging blocks of stone. I'm not much of an actor, but I managed to get a few smiles.

'Grace. What's the one thing Grace does really well and loves to do a lot of?'

'Talk.' The class erupted in laughter.

'That's not as funny as it sounds,' I said. 'There are so many businesses which require the ability to communicate. There are the obvious ones, such as sales, public relations, public speaking, human resources. But use your imagination. If Cathy loves to talk and does it well, she is sitting on a potential goldmine.'

'I just thought of something!' Margaret leapt to her feet. 'I know what I'm good at!'

'What's that?' I was surprised by her sudden enthusiasm.

'I'm — I mean Margaret — is good at finding out where to buy things. She loves the hunt. She thrives on it.'

'Well done. Any idea how she will do that once and sell it many times?'

'She could set up a sourcing business. You only have to find something once to know where it is the next time.'

'She's right, you know.' Mitch says. 'She's the world's most experienced shopper.'

These sudden moments of understanding or personal insight are such rewarding moments for teachers and facilitators — it's rare for us to forget the sight of the light coming on.

Rule 7: Your friends are not your network.

'You've probably heard someone say that we are all living magnets. Now the law of electromagnetic force is that like forces repel each other and unlike forces attract. Sorry to bring physics into it again, but if we are living magnets, we should be attracting opposites, not people who are the same as us.

'Networking, therefore, is not about attracting people who think like you do, or who offer the same services as you. That's inviting competition. Networking is gathering around you people who fill a need you have, and vice versa.

> True networks are made up of people who are different from you.

'A network consists of interdependent relationships. Each node in the network has a specific value to add to the effectiveness of the whole network. Therefore true networkers seek out people who complement them, not people who mirror them. Each person in your network should bring something different to the equation.

'Have you ever noticed that successful people generally know the right person to go to when there is a specific need? Why is that? Because they have made a conscious effort to extend their supplier base. I know it sounds cynical to treat people as a supplier base or a potential customer base, but it's a very real picture of effective networking.'

'That's gross,' Grace said. 'I can't use people for what I can get out of them.'

'Of course you can't. Not in your personal life. You can't use your friends. But you have to differentiate between your friends and your network. In terms of profit and loss, your friends are probably neutral. Most of the time they don't add much to the power of your network. I am not saying they are worthless, or that they don't fill your life with love and kindness. These are not issues we deal with when we are focusing on wealth creation. As wonderful as they are, friendships do not normally help you grow your earning potential. In pure, beastly, nasty, clinical, cold, cynical, materialistic terms, your friends do not add one iota to the growth of your financial independence.'

'That makes sense,' Cathy said. 'You don't make friends so that they can help you make money.'

'Precisely. And that is the difference between networking and friendship. I go out with my friends. We go to dinner, have a few drinks, talk about the footie, discuss our families, etc. We have a good time. It's an important way to relax and feel wanted. But it really doesn't matter how good they make me feel about myself when I go home and look at the balance sheet of my financial life. Friends might build my self-worth, but generally they do very little for my net worth.'

> Friends do not generally help you build your net worth; your network does that.

'Grace is finding it hard to think in such materialistic terms,' Grace said.

'Why? We live in a material world. We want to have enough money to first enjoy that material world, and

> *Your financial adviser is not your friend; you need their advice, not their friendship.*

then to set ourselves free from it so we can enter a deeper, more meaningful world. At this stage in your life, I suggest that freedom from this material matrix starts with listening to the most materialistic of all people in your network — your bank manager, your accountant or your financial adviser. None of these is your friend. Thank heavens. You don't need sympathy. You need facts and figures.'

'Toney, you're talking about a dog-eat-dog world,' Andy said. 'You can't be that cynical.'

'I'm not cynical. I just know the difference between money and emotion, between my network and my friends. I love my friends and my family, but I don't love the people in my financial network. What's love got to do with it? We are honest with each other. We help each other, not because of some high-sounding moral code, but because we're involved in mutually beneficial transactions. You do something for me and I will do something for you.'

Cathy and Grace sighed, almost simultaneously.

> *Your personal life is not a question of facts and figures, but your financial life is.*

'I know it's a bit of shock therapy, but I think we can all do with a dose of it. All this talk about billable hours, personal timesheets, your own unique selling propositions, is not because I want to reduce your personal life to a matter of facts and figures, but because I want to reduce your financial life to a matter of facts and figures.'

'Now, can anyone sum up what I've been saying?'

'Your friends are not your network. The rules of friendship are very different from the rules of networking,' Margaret said. 'Margaret can handle that.'

For a long time I have suspected that the one thing that stops people from honestly looking at where they are in life and where they want to be has much to do with the emotional gumbo in which they're floundering. It was thus time for my next trick.

I reached into my bag of goodies and withdrew a battered rolodex. As I flipped through the hundreds of business cards (they weren't real, of course — I keep a PDA now), I said, 'This is my network.'

Then I reached in and took out the slimmest possible volume that I could find at the stationer's that morning.

'And these are my friends.' I pretended to look hard for entries, just to add to the dramatic effect.

It got a laugh.

Rule 8: Think of everything as being for sale.

'And now for the next rule. Absolutely everything is for sale. Look around you. There is not one thing that could not find its way to market. Even most non-material things are also theoretically for sale. Of course that's not the same thing as saying you should sell them. I am simply pointing out that Rich Matrix thinking is different from Bitch Matrix thinking.

'I once looked around my living room and thought it would be an interesting exercise to put a price tag on every item, as if I was going to hold a huge garage sale. It struck me that I had only a very sketchy knowledge of the price of these things. Obviously, their monetary value was no longer important to me. The reason I couldn't put a price tag on them was simple: I hadn't bought them to sell and I didn't need to sell them.

'So I thought to myself, *What if I were so desperate that the sale of the contents of my house meant the difference between eating and starving?* Then I would really need to sell these things. And what happens when you really need to sell something? You probably take whatever price you can get for it.

'But there was one item I knew the price of. It was a piece of art by a local artist who had grown in reputation over the years. Why do you think I knew the price?'

'Obviously, because you wanted to sell it one day,' Andy said.

'Exactly. I wanted to sell it. And what happens when you're not desperate to sell, but you want to sell in order to make a return on an investment?'

'You go for the highest price on offer,' Andy answered.

> Work at increasing the value of what you're selling.

'Andy is on the ball. Now let's draw a parallel with the services or products or talents we are going to sell to make money. If you're working just to fulfil your needs, you will not get much. You will accept what's on offer and match your needs with that. If you are working to increase the value of what you already have, however, you are likely to go for, and get, a lot more.'

'You've lost me,' Cathy said.

'Well, let's introduce another rule to help explain the difference between need and want.'

Rule 9: Never increase your needs as your income increases.

'Let's say Cathy makes $50,000 this year. She tells us that she needs that much to live on, which means she has very little left over. If she makes $100,000 next year, she would — I guess — probably say she needs all of that as well. Her work — the selling of her time and skills — is going only towards fulfilling her needs. My guess is that the more she earns, the more she will need. That is not very financially intelligent. She is letting her needs expand with her income.

'Financial intelligence says that you never get wealthy by growing your needs as you grow your income. Wealth comes by either reducing your needs or maintaining them as your income increases.

'It's very simple. Work out what you need, and how much you need to work to pay for that. If you receive anything beyond that for the work you do, invest it so that it grows in value. Over time you will build up capital, which means you will be less desperate to sell your skills and services for whatever you can get and more able to get a higher return for them.'

> Determine how much money you need; spend that and invest the rest.

Rule 10: Everything is negotiable.

'Not only should you look at everything as if it could be sold for a higher price than it was bought for; you should also live with the belief that everything is negotiable.

'I remember joining a gym with a friend of mine. When I joined I paid the standard membership fee. When he joined, he not only paid much less than I did, but also walked away with every piece of promotional merchandise the club had to offer. What was his secret? It was simple. He started with the belief that everything was negotiable, and used all his natural charm and negotiating skills to get what he wanted.

'We have some odd beliefs in our society. First, we think it's wrong to ask for a discount. Somehow we believe that this is only culturally appropriate in the third world. Second, we think it's wrong to haggle over the price. Again, that's what they do in other societies, not ours. Do you know what these attitudes actually do? They undermine the power of the purchaser to determine price. Companies charge only what people are willing to pay. If we're so dumb that we pay whatever they ask for, we deserve to be ripped off.

'The reason I bring this rule to your attention is because it's about power.

> Negotiate from a position of want, not need.

You've heard the expression, "the rich and powerful"? Have you ever heard the expression "the poor and powerful"? It doesn't work, does it? Having money is always the stronger side of the transaction, because if you are in that position, you are coming from want, not need. The distance between those two positions is what I like to call the rich man's power voltage. In other words, if you enter a transaction *needing* a certain outcome, you are in a weak position. If you enter a transaction *wanting* a certain outcome but not needing it, you can bargain from a position of power.

'To sum up, we could say that in any negotiation, the rich can always walk away; they can always go somewhere else. The poor, however, have little choice.'

'But this doesn't actually apply until we are actually rich, does it?' Margaret asked.

'Yes it does. You can start thinking like this, and acting like someone in the Rich Matrix, straight away. If

> Start flexing your consumer muscles.

you need a loaf of bread, there is not much you can do but pay the advertised price. But if you want a new television, try negotiating for it. Get a feel for the strategic advantage you have simply because you *want* something rather than *need* it. And it's not just about saving a few bucks; it's about being in control — in this case, of market forces.

'You don't have to be moving millions of dollars in the stock market to exercise control over the market. Every time you take advantage of your own purchasing power, you are exerting a measure of control.

'But I should also point out that the art of negotiation is a learned skill. It's not just about self-confidence. It has its own set of rules, and they are worth learning. Really good negotiation is as strategically complicated as a good game of chess. It has to do with the interplay of power, knowledge and benefit. I suggest you take a course in negotiating skills before you start selling your services.'

Rule 11: Knowledge is power, so strive to know more.

'Money is power. True. But then so is knowledge. If you know more, you are stronger. It doesn't matter if you're making paper aeroplanes for a living, you have to be one step ahead of everyone else. Progress, whether personal or financial, is about moving ahead, finding ways to be more productive, more creative and more competitive. This philosophy is taught to companies repeatedly, and it's just as valid for the individual.

'I've kept this rule to the end of the session, because it is a call to yet another commitment. What I have found disturbing is that so many people who work hard for their money know very little about what they can do with it. Why? Because they don't commit to studying it.

'The subject of money is enormous — you could study investment, insurance, accounting, finance, the share market, superannuation, property, just for a start — so plan for a lifetime of learning.

> Study money as a foreign language: learn its vocabulary and usage, and how to read it, listen to it and speak it.

'Over the remaining two weeks of this course you'll be thinking about the power of promises. One of the best promises you can make is to commit yourself to study one aspect of money or wealth creation. So, bearing in mind everything I have said so far, can anyone tell me how best to learn about money?'

'Make a specific promise to study a specific aspect of money at a specific time,' Andy said.

'Great.'

'Make that promise unbreakable,' Grace added. 'And *really, really* want to.'

'Zero-option,' Cathy added.

'Love it or leave it,' Phil said. 'Either/or thinking.'

'This is all very reassuring. You've been listening. But can anyone tell me what's the most important rule to follow with regard to knowledge?'

'You haven't told us that one yet, Toney,' Margaret said with a cheeky smile.

'OK. The knowledge rule is *Use it or lose it*. So if knowledge is power, what do you think the power rule is?'

'Use it or lose it,' they said in chorus.

'And what do you think the cardinal rule of money is?'

'Use it or lose it,' returned the chorus.

To end the evening, I wrote on the whiteboard:

> KNOWLEDGE: USE IT OR LOSE IT.
> POWER: USE IT OR LOSE IT.
> MONEY: USE IT OR LOSE IT.

'Learn these principles,' I said. 'Learn them, live them and grow rich.'

10. The rulebook of the rich: Part 2

'There's lots of advice around about what makes a person free. One of the most common suggestions is that work makes you free. When I first heard that I asked myself, free from what? How does work make you free? It enslaves you for eight hours or more a day. How could it possibly make you free?'

Rule 12: Labour less, work more.

'If you work in order to live, which is unfortunately what most of us do, then of course work is something you will want to be free from, rather than something that makes you free.

'It's time to call in the mythbusters. When the industrial revolution took people away from the land and put them into factories, to become part of the machinery of production, work and life had to be divorced. One of the rights workers fought for was scheduled

> Work is not what you are paid to do; that's labour.

155

time off. This eventually led to the ludicrous idea that work is a necessary evil for which you get paid, and your life is what you do when you're not working. In other words, what you get paid for is work; what you don't get paid for is life.

'This is clearly not useful. How can we undo this idea? First, we need to distinguish between labour and your life-work. If someone else can do it, or if a computer can do it, it's labour. It might be valuable, necessary and purposeful, but it's still labour. Whether you're a highly paid executive or a lowly paid factory hand, if someone else pays you for the work you do, it's labour.

'But what happens if that labour happens to coincide with your defining ability? Imagine how happy and productive you would be at work if your labour and your life-work were the same! It's uncommon, of course, since the reality is that we all have to pay our own way through life and generally do this by being paid for our labour.

'The marriage between labour and your life-work is an ideal. It's not the only way to grow wealthy, naturally, but if it happens, it certainly helps.

'We are told to live a balanced life, separating work and leisure. However, I suspect that for some (not everyone, of course) there is a great sense of fulfilment when work and life are inseparable; when they flow into each other.

'This doesn't mean that you spend all day at the computer, or that instead of going to your kid's football match you head to the office. It doesn't even mean that you take your work problems home.

'My proposition is that your work should define you as much as your role as a father, mother, sports coach or golfer does. You don't step from one role into another; you don't live separate roles. You are indivisible.

'This approach to work is only possible if you do work that is authentically you, that flows naturally from your talents and your ambitions. For the sake of clarity we will call this your life-work. Your life-work is not nine-to-five labour; that is for slaves.

'The slave mentality, the narrow view of work as labour, runs through our workplace training, urging us, the human components of the master workflow plan, to ever higher levels of efficiency and productivity. While all that makes a certain kind of economic sense, it will not make you rich.

'For most people, this is a difficult concept, because it challenges our conventional view of work. It takes a lot of courage to step outside the run-of-the-mill moneymaking machinery and start your own life-work.

'What are some good work habits?' I asked.

Andy was first to answer.

'Making to-do lists and priority lists.'

'Does Andy stick to his to-do lists?'

'No.'

> Your life-work is the expression of your defining talent.

'What about dealing with procrastination by breaking down projects into less overwhelming tasks?' asked Margaret.

'An excellent textbook answer, Margaret. Anyone else?'

'Giving oneself incentives,' Mitch said.

'I suppose Mitch does that all the time?'

'No.'

'Then why say it?'

'Because it's what everyone says.'

Grace added her bit.

'We have to eliminate bad habits that waste time. Avoid distractions,' she said.

I rolled my eyes.

'What you are all giving me are the sort of statements made by bosses, who are no more than

> So-called good work habits are often just good office administration.

machine operators in suits. Do you think that the rich actually do any of what you said? Do you think that those who are doing their life-work sit down every day to draw up lists, using different coloured pens to mark priorities, check off their diaries religiously, set goals and give themselves rewards, breaking their work down into manageable pieces? Do you really think they do this?

'Perhaps reasonably well-paid managers do. Perhaps the sales manager of the year does. But not the really rich. They get others to do all that for them.'

The class was puzzled. With all I had said about time management and goal-setting, they had probably been expecting a traditional take on work habits.

'What you have been talking about is good office management. What I am asking you to do is to take a completely different approach.'

Cathy and Grace turned towards each other and shrugged their shoulders.

> Work habits dull the mind. Look for ways to work differently.

'Let me ask you another question. What is the downside to habit?'

'You end up doing the same thing in the same way again and again,' Andy said.

'Right. And that leads to stagnation. It locks you into yet another paradigm. You see, to-do lists and the like are fine, but when you sit down to make them you bring a ready-made structure to them — what you have always done. If it has taken you one week in the past to complete a project, it is going to take you one week next time as well. Try something different. Try to do it in half the time. Or if someone tells you that the only way to sell your product is by doing such and such, listen, but then look for a different and better way to do it.

'As long as you separate your work into eight hours a day, break down each of those hours into minutes, and lock yourself into that, you aren't giving yourself a chance to produce your best. This is no way to engage in your life-work.

'What is to stop you leaping out of bed, with an idea in your head, and jotting it down? Oh, of course. You're not supposed to do that. The alarm is set for seven o'clock. Or what is to stop you from getting great ideas just by watching your children at play — they are always a great inspiration?

'If what you are doing does not inspire you, it's just labour. However, if your work flows from your life, if it is inseparable from who you are, you have the potential to do great things.

Rule 13: The 80/20 rule is for machines — bad ones.

'I'm sure you have all heard about the 80/20 rule: 80 per cent of what you achieve comes from 20 per cent of your effort. Now I don't know what scientific data is available to prove that, but I suspect that the rule is rubbish, carrying only the authority of repetition. Does anyone have any thoughts on this rule?'

'Well, they say you should look for the 20 per cent and really throw your effort into that,' Andy said.

'True, but what happens when you throw your effort into it?'

'Well, obviously it becomes more than 20 per cent,' Margaret said.

'Yep. So what is the ideal?'

'Make 100 per cent of your effort related to 100 per cent of your output,' Phil said.

Phil had beaten me to it, again.

'That's probably not possible, because it would be pretty exhausting, wouldn't it? But the direction is right, and it is in line with our *really, really* principle, our idea of zero-option decision-making. In short, follow the 100/100 rule.'

'You're going to turn us into fanatics, Toney,' Cathy said. 'You've got to have a break from your work some time.'

'I didn't say you couldn't break from what you are doing. I am saying that you can't break from your life-work, because it is your life. Being obsessed by something doesn't necessarily mean that you spend all your time going on about it, but it does mean that you spend all your time open to it. Turn your brain off, we are told. Relax. Think of something else for a while. That's another myth I'd like to eradicate. As if your brain can be turned off! It's working even while you sleep. While you're out there on the ski slopes, or watering your garden, or playing with your children, you are still you, and part of that you is your brain at its life-work, inventing, creating, drawing up blueprints. When you sit down to watch TV, if you are in *really, really* mode, even something as mind-numbing as a soapie can bring an idea into your head. This is what I mean by your life-work. When your life and your life-work are one and the same, you cannot turn either off.'

Rule 14: Face your fears and tell them to wait.

'Andy is a bit scared of this approach. Conventional work structures make him feel secure,' Andy said.

'Face this fear head on,' I said. 'I remember, as a little boy, being frightened by phantoms, ghosts, spiders, or bogeymen — I don't remember what they were, exactly. My father taught me how to deal with all these creatures. He told me to simply turn to them and ask them to wait a while, until I was ready to be frightened. They could scare me as much as they like,

I would say to them, but they would just have to sit in the corner of my room and wait until the morning. I promised to be really frightened then. Of course when morning came they had cleared out, so I couldn't keep that particular promise. I use the same strategy to deal with fears in my adult life.

'We have already spoken about the Choice Gap. We have said that to be in control of your life you have to step into that Choice Gap, pause, and then choose the way you react. Such control is characteristic behaviour in the Rich Matrix. It is especially important when you are making decisions relating to being rich — few people have become rich by being impulsive — and when dealing with fear and worry. Try to deal with fears by using the Choice Gap. Stand face to face with your fear and say something like, "Yes, I am scared that this is not going to work, but I will only be scared at 4.30 pm this afternoon. And then I will really be scared." Ask your fears to sit in the corner until you are ready. Then when 4.30 pm comes, you can go into scared mode. Obviously, your fear just fizzles out.'

> Make an appointment with your fears and keep it.

'You can't be serious, Toney!' Margaret said.

'Deadly serious. Try it with even a small worry. I know a public speaker who does it all the time. She allows herself to get really frightened one hour before she is due to speak, and only for 10 minutes. She tells herself that she can really go to town on her fears and they can mess up her talk as much as they like, but they have to wait until exactly one hour before. She even sets her mobile phone alarm to go off. I will never forget her telling me, "Excuse me, but it's now time to be frightened." It's the Choice Gap. It's the difference between letting your fears control you and controlling them yourself.

'Cathy, what's Cathy biggest fear about starting her own catering business?'

'Cathy, of course, is worried that it will be a flop, that she will lose her money and be in debt and ...'

'A whole menu of fears,' I interrupted.

'So what is Cathy supposed to do? They're not just going to go away, you know.'

'No. But they will do what they are told. My suggestion is that you have two small fear sessions each day, at exactly the same time every day. In other words, at 8.25 am and 5.35 pm you let your fears have the floor. It's their time. You have promised it to them and you should keep your promise. So whenever you have a fear rise unexpectedly during the day, just tell it to wait until the appointed time. Then when the time comes, drop whatever you're doing and have your fear sessions.'

| Fears, thoughts and feelings can be made to wait. |

'Hmm. That might work for a diet,' Grace said. It always amused me how Grace turned everything back to her weight problem.

'Actually, Grace, I know someone who does exactly that. More to do with her self-image, actually.'

'You would,' Margaret said cynically.

'Well, believe it or not. She was plump. There was no point denying that. But that was, in my opinion, not relevant. She actually hated herself in her body. She thought she was ugly. So she tried the delayed reaction technique. She would sit in front of the mirror once a day at exactly the same time and let loose all the self-hating thoughts she had had that day. Of course by the time her appointment with herself came around, those thoughts had long gone.

| Don't try to change negative thoughts into positive ones; just set aside a time to have them. |

'We said that 80 per cent of our time was probably unproductive. Well, I'd bet anything that most of it is spent in thoughts — fears, doubts, worries —

that could be told to behave themselves until we were ready. So when you sit down to launch yourself into a project and you start thinking about all the things that will go wrong, don't try to suppress these thoughts. Just allocate a particular time to have them.'

'It all sounds a bit simple,' Margaret said.

'Why doesn't Margaret hold that thought — that it is childish, stupid and whatever — until 9.15 this evening?'

She took her mobile phone.

'I'll set the alarm now.'

It took us all a few minutes to stop laughing.

'I've got something even funnier to tell you,' I said, reaching for my notes. 'Here is the kind of thing you read from the so-called gurus. *Write down three things that have worried you lately. Think about the worst possible outcome for each of your three worries. Now write down the realistic outcomes for those same three worries. Contrast the realistic outcomes with the worst-case scenarios. Once you are aware of the facts, you can see that the odds are against the worst-case scenario ever happening. Repeat this exercise anytime you feel worried.* As if anyone is going to go to all that trouble! That's just upgrading your worries from a Category 3 storm to a Category 5 cyclone. All that nonsense is based on the assumption that your fears are rational, which means you can reason yourself out of them. Fears are forces; they're not arguments, so you will never defeat them with arguments. So let your fears have their way with you, because they won't go away. But let that happen when you are ready to let it happen. No one is fearless. Rather, those who control their lives also control their fears.'

> Your fears are not rational, so you can't be reasonable with them.

Rule 15: Manage risk.

'Risk management sounds terribly technical, doesn't it? It's actually just another way of gaining more control over the events that shape your life. It's about knowing when to seize an opportunity and when to let one go. Once you admit that any action, especially a business endeavour, involves risk — that is, it has unintended consequences as well as intended ones — you will see that the main principle of risk management is simple: doing something will either increase or decrease the odds of a positive outcome. This is Newton's second law at work: Doing the right something will bring about the right outcome.

'Professional risk managers are paid very well for applying Newton's second law; they evaluate what the risks of any situation are and then decide what action will raise the odds of a positive outcome.

'However, if you think about it, you're all pretty adept at being risk managers all day, every day. There's a risk in everything you do, and you reduce the risk of negative outcomes through the way you walk, the way you sit, the clothing you wear, the food you eat. All your activities are, or theoretically should be, geared towards achieving the best outcomes for you.

> You have been learning to manage risk since you were born.

'If I tell you to cross the highway, you will use a pedestrian crossing because you believe you have a better chance of getting safely across this way than by trying to slip through speeding traffic. You have a pair of lungs, and there are certain odds that if you smoke cigarettes you will lose your lungs, and your whole self, to cancer. The deliberate action you need in this case to reduce

> You manage risk by defining a negative outcome and taking action to avoid it.

your odds is pretty obvious: don't smoke. Now these are very obvious negative outcomes, but they illustrate a basic principle of risk management: first define the negative outcome you wish to avoid. In these examples, you don't want to be flattened by a car and you don't want to get lung cancer.

'In other words, define your input by looking at your output — start with the end in mind, as one of Stephen Covey's *Seven Habits of Highly Effective People* puts it.

'Look back from the future before you make any decision that has to do with money. That is a very powerful principle, and wealthy people, who are wealthy because they build their wealth by managing risk, apply it religiously.'

> Look back from the future before you make a decision.

'Doesn't it pay to sometimes just "have a go"?'

'Sorry, Mitch, but only a fool just "has a go". Have you ever seen professional card players at work? Lady Luck is as mythical as Santa Claus.

'Consider what professional poker players — professional risk-takers — do: they count their cards. They are constantly aware of the odds of certain outcomes. They could, of course, just close their eyes and hope that the right cards are mysteriously thrown their way, but they wouldn't last long. Professional gamblers deliberately increase their odds of winning — and therefore also reduce their odds of losing — by managing the risk involved in a wager. There is not much difference between this and being a good stock trader or investment adviser.

'I believe that we can bring the principle of risk management into our daily lives. Can anyone think where we might start?'

'Well, doing something is Newton's first law, isn't it?' Another gold star for Phil.

'Yes, but the second law is more appropriate here — Do the right something. Is anyone here a victim of compulsive behaviour?'

'Mitch is,' Mitch said. Margaret threw a dagger at him.

'Does Mitch want to tell us what that is?'

'No,' he said, shifting uncomfortably in his seat. I could almost hear everyone's imagination shift a gear.

'OK. Let's pretend, then, that Mitch is a compulsive daydreamer. He spends far too much time tripping off into his own fantasy world. He is, in other words, a compulsive escapist.' It was the most harmless addiction I could think of.

'What would Mitch do in order to reduce the risk of daydreaming and increase the risk of doing something productive?'

Mitch shrugged his shoulders. Obviously, he was not addicted to daydreaming.

'He could put himself in situations where the risk of falling into one of his daydreams was much lower,' Margaret suggested, as if coming to his defence. Clearly, there was a secret they both wanted to keep.

'I suppose he could change his environment, look for things that physically distract him or bring on a reverie and remove them. Or he could do what I taught you to do with fears. If he dreams about sailing around the world, he could reduce the risk of that taking up his mind by giving it a time slot. He could then look forward to sunny climes and stretches of blue ocean between 5.10 pm and 5.30 pm every evening. Whenever he feels a daydream coming on, all he has to do is tell it to wait. He would not be denying his pleasure; he would just be delaying it. Of course by the time 5.10 comes around he would probably have lost the desire to pull up the anchor and cast off. He has therefore done something to reduce the risk of becoming a victim to his compulsive behaviour.

'Remember this: risk, like fear, will not go away. There is a risk that a meteor will fall out of the sky and put a quick end to this session. It's a small risk, but it's always there. There's a risk that your house will burn down, or that

> Risks cannot be made to disappear; they can only be reduced or increased.

you will be liable for a massive workers' compensation payout. None of these risks will go away just because you ignore them.

'We do not know whether or not these things will occur. Nor can we ever be certain about the outcome of our actions. But we can calculate the odds of a positive or negative outcome.

'Professional financial planners and risk assessors use simulations to examine different outcomes, to see how different investment portfolios might perform in

> You cannot know outcomes, but you can know their odds.

different market conditions. They can then measure the risk of an investment strategy. Notice that they don't do away with risk; they just keep it under control.

'These days, when we are no longer assured of a job for life or a generous government handout when we're in the autumn of our lives, looking at the risks of where we are going has become more important than ever.

'I am not just talking about risk in terms of things like investment portfolios. I am talking about the risks involved in continuing to behave the way you are behaving, or maintaining the thinking patterns that have been keeping you from fulfilling yourself. Remember the Bridget Jones Syndrome?

> Consider the risk of continuing with inappropriate behaviour.

Well, now you have to ask yourself, what is the risk of zero growth if I continue to do such and such? Risk management, in other words, is about the decisions you make (or don't make) in your normal life.

'So can anyone tell me, in a sentence, the best way to manage risks — financial or otherwise?'

'Do something to reduce the odds of something bad happening.'

Phil again.

Rule 16: Seek out the influential and influence them.

'You've all heard of Dale Carnegie's book *How to Win Friends and Influence People*. I must confess, I've never read it. I have never been able to get past the title — it says so much that I am still learning its implications. Can anyone suggest, from what we have learned so far, how I would change the title?'

I was expecting Phil to come up with the right answer. Instead, Grace took the lead. 'Your friends are not your network. It should read *How to Create a Network and Influence People*.'

'Bravo, Grace. That's right. What sort of friends would you be making if the basis of your friendship were how much influence they had? And when they can no longer be used to advance you, what do you do? Dump them?

> No one ever grew rich by being an island.

'Separate your friends from your network. No man is an island, they say, and no one ever grew rich by isolating themselves and influencing no one. How could you? How could you possibly make money alone on a deserted island? Money is the product of a network — commerce between goods, services and labour. It doesn't grow by itself. It's circulated throughout a network.

'I once saw a man go to an ATM machine and put on a pair of gloves before he touched it. Obviously, he had a few psychological problems. I wondered if he also used a pair of gloves when he handled that money — a lot more germ-ridden fingers would have held those notes than pressed the buttons on an ATM machine.

'The point is that money circulates. It's constantly on the move.

'To get more of it you need to be in a network, and there are very simple rules for winning people over to your network. I don't want to go on about how to be nice to people, how to give them what they want, not judge them, yada yada yada.

'How to win people over to your side is just common sense. It doesn't take a bestselling book to know that someone to whom you provide what they want is going to be a lot more supportive to you than someone whose favourite pet you just poisoned. Nor does it take an Einstein to realise that the more someone likes you or the better you treat someone the more likely you are going to make a sale. I don't understand why we have to have whole courses on such fundamental and self-evident truths.

'Proactively seeking out influential people is not difficult. Can anyone suggest how we win influential people over to our network?'

'Cathy doesn't know any influential people.'

'Cathy works in a café and doesn't know any influential people? Is Cathy serious?'

Cathy looked stunned.

'Of all the people in this room, Cathy is more likely than anyone to have a healthy network of contacts. Why doesn't she, then?'

'She has never treated her customers as potential contacts,' Cathy said a little defiantly.

'Why not? Imagine if Cathy had just spent a minute which each of her customers, made them feel important, taken their business cards, remembered

A business card is a necessary tool for spreading your influence.

them by name when they came in, given them a little extra service. She might end up with a thousand business cards at the end of the year, and probability says that at least some of those business cards might make all the difference to her. What about her own business card?'

'She doesn't have one.'

'What? A business card is an essential tool. Not just a business card with your name and contact details on it, but a business card that says *specifically* what you can do for someone; what you bring to a network. Many of the business cards you see aren't much use. It's no wonder they get thrown out. It's never enough to have the company you work for or the name of your business on one side. On one side, at least, you should also carry a statement of what you can offer. The question in the mind of the recipient is, *What can this person do for me or my business?* Your business card should give them a ready-made answer so that they don't have to ask you. If you can't think of the answer, you probably have nothing to sell.'

> Your business card must state what you bring to the network of influence.

I reached into my pocket and showed them a business card.

'This card is from a web designer. After I read it, I thought, *So what? What makes you different from the thousand web designers in the yellow pages? What can you do for me that no one else can? What is your USP?'*

> Your business card must carry your USP.

'But don't most people just throw these cards in the bin?' Grace asked.

'Not me. That's a waste of trees — and of talent. You know what I do with all the business cards I get? When I get home, I send an email — to no matter

> Follow up on all business cards you are given.

who it is — to thank them for the opportunity of meeting them. I even do it for people I never expect to meet again, because of the simple fact that in life, one never knows.

'Everyone likes to feel important. A sentence just acknowledging someone's existence is worth a thousand cold calls. So remember this: everyone, absolutely everyone, is a potential member of your network, an associate member of your sales force.

> Everyone is a potential member of your sales force.

'And here is a truth we want to forget because for some reason we think it's ugly.

'You don't make money. The Federal Treasury and the Mint do that. You accumulate money by taking it from someone else and then getting it to grow.

> You don't make money. You take it.

That's why networking — throwing your net out into the sea of potential money-givers — is absolutely essential to making money.'

'Since there is a finite amount of money in circulation, the more you have the less someone else has. I know that sounds very crude, but it's the way the money system works. It's also the reason why it's simply not possible for everyone to grow rich.

'However, the fact that you grow rich by taking it from someone else in the system doesn't have to be a source of guilt. It can also be a source of a serious social responsibility.

'One of the most generous philanthropists of recent years is Bill Gates, the founder of Microsoft and one of the richest people in the world. If the interviews are to be believed, he gets as much joy giving money as he does making it. There's a lot to be said for being able to afford generosity.'

Rule 17: Work at your financial literacy.

My next rule came along with a surprise.

'I asked Phil to take a picture of his home library for me. Here it is.'

I projected the photo onto the whiteboard.

'I can read many of the titles. There's a whole range of books here: Shakespeare, John Grisham, cookbooks, biographies of sporting heroes, a gardening book, a few naughty ones (judging from their titles), and a set of encyclopaedias. Oh Phil, how you can use a hardcover encyclopaedia in the 21st century?'

The class found this as amusing as I did.

Can anyone suggest what's odd about Phil's library?'

After a pause, I answered my own question: 'There are no books on money. When I saw this, I had to ask myself whether or not Phil was really interested in money.

'If you want to make money, you must be prepared to learn about it. It's a game, and every game has its rules. It's also an art, and every art has its methods. It's also a science, and every science has its principles. It's also a language, with a specialised vocabulary. So if you really do want to build wealth, you have to study money.

> If you want to live in a world of money, you must learn about it.

'I'm not asking you to enrol in a Masters in Financial Planning. It is not academic knowledge you need; it's literacy.

'How many of you skip the business section in the newspaper?'

All raised their hands, even Phil and Andy.

'I can't believe it!' I said with genuine surprise. 'How many of you have educational books on personal investing, the basics of the stock market or how-to guides for property investment?'

'Cathy has a few get-rich books,' Cathy said.

'So does Andy.'

'That's not what I'm talking about. I am talking about useful knowledge that can help you make sensible decisions about money.

'You all have work to do. To cut a long search short, here are what I consider the three commandments of money-making:

1   Think, don't feel.
2   Grow your money, don't save it.
3   Expect the worst so you can enjoy the best.

'Let's look at the first commandment. *Think, don't feel*.

'I think it is fair to say that some of the least flamboyant people in the world are money managers. You don't become a bank chairman because you're a lot of fun to be with. You get there because you're cold, calculating, mean, disciplined and most of all, unfeeling ... at least when you have to be. When it comes to money, think like they do. Put on the pin-stripe suit of an investment manager. Pore over those tedious prospectuses with the same enthusiasm as you would feel for a page-turning novel. Think about possible returns — don't have a feeling about them. That means getting out a calculator and crunching the numbers. It also means being critical of everything you read — especially packages designed to arouse your feelings. Always remember what I said at the beginning of the course: you are not a person in the world of money, you are an account number, nothing more than a potential debtor or creditor.

'Don't be wooed by nice people. They want your money. Period. So get into the habit of thinking your way through their offerings.

'It requires a lot of self-discipline to be a prudent investor. Often it involves waiting — standing on the

> Prudent investment involves waiting at the Choice Gap before making a decision.

edge of our Choice Gap — until the right moment comes along. And you will know it's the right moment not because you feel it, but because you have used your knowledge and skills to work out what is the right moment.'

'How on earth are we going to learn that?' Cathy asked.

'It's like anything else that you have to learn. You get a teacher and you begin taking your first small steps. With enough practice you end up walking by yourself. You will learn to diversify, spreading your money across different classes of assets and industries. You will learn to read the pulse of the financial markets, to understand and discriminate between different dividend policies, and to pay attention to fees and taxes.'

'Whoa,' said Grace. 'This is all too much.'

'They're only words, Grace, and words have meanings which we can learn. Don't be put off just because you don't know them yet. In fact, be turned on because you don't know. There's a whole new world waiting for all of you.

'Lots of people try to use specialised language to impress us: doctors use big words, lawyers throw in a bit of Latin, and technicians bamboozle us with nerd-speak. It's only a sales pitch, and they're only words. I have met doctors, lawyers and technicians whose basic intelligence I question, but they sound impressive because I don't know the meaning of the words they use. If I learned their vocabulary, they would have less power over me. The same is true for finance experts. Learn their language and you'll soon be able to tell the difference between one who knows and one who pretends to know.

'The second rule is fairly straightforward: *Grow your money, don't save it*. This simply means you won't get rich by putting your money in a bank and earning interest from an ordinary savings account. You have to think of money as something that grows best in certain places. Remember, there are only three things you can do with money: you can spend it, save it, or grow it. If you are serious about making money, you will look for ways to grow it.

> You have three choices when you have $100 in your hand: spend it, save it, or grow it.

'The final rule for the wise investor is: *Expect the worst so you can enjoy the best.* This just means always to keep some cash on hand. People are no different from companies in that they need liquidity to run their daily lives and to cope with emergencies.

'Cash is not, of course, the only way to protect yourself against the unexpected; insurance is the other. When I hear about people who don't take out insurance to protect their most valuable assets — their health and homes, for example — I think of it not so much as

> Having no insurance is as senseless as it is arrogant.

an act of defining stupidity, but as an act of unreasonable arrogance. It's rooted in the belief that somehow they are exempt from the surprises of life. Wrong. Even the Queen had a fire in Windsor Palace. I'm sure Her Majesty wasted no time in telling some hapless insurance broker the bad news.

'Insurance is also a form of investment, so it too has to be studied, with plans and prices compared, advice taken, decisions made.'

'Sounds like we have weeks of study ahead of us,' Grace said.

'A lifetime, Grace, a lifetime learning about money, if you really, really want to be rich. Of course, if you really, really want something else, then if I were you I'd spend my time learning about that.'

Rule 18: Manage your debt.

'What happens in a business when an employee is completely unmanageable; when he or she doesn't respond to directions no matter how hard the manager tries?'

'They get the sack,' Margaret said.

'Right. You just get rid of what you can't manage. But what happens to debt?'

'It doesn't go away until you pay it back,' Mitch said.

'In other words, no matter how unmanageable your debt has become, it can't just be made to disappear. And it's alive: it grows every day. So you have to either kill it off or manage it. If you're going to manage it, you might as well do it before it reaches a critical stage.'

'Having no debt whatsoever is not necessarily a good thing, as anyone who has ever borrowed money for a house and watched the value of the house shoot up will tell you. But debt that grows without bearing any fruit is like a poisonous weed. It will kill the rest of your garden, and undermine the foundations of your financial future.'

I looked around the room for a victim. 'Let's ask Andy to show us the cards he has in his pocket.'

'Andy has two credit cards, a bank card and a charge card.'

'Does Andy have to pay the charge card off every month?

'Yes.'

'And the credit cards?'

'No. Monthly minimum repayments only.'

'Which means that the bank card and the charge card are self-managing. They do not grow. The credit cards, on the other hand, are growing more and more out of control every day.

'Credit card companies are making money from you even while you're asleep. Of course there are situations for which we need credit cards — and some have to be paid off in full every month — but most of them just burn holes in our wallets.'

'So what do we do with credit cards?' Andy asked.

'Don't use them unless you have to. Don't feed them unless you have no other choice. If you starve them they will die. Keep them manageable.'

Rule 19: Get ready for your autumn.

'The next rule is a serious one. I have never understood why people avoid thinking about their retirement, or the inevitability of their own death. Unless you plan to do away with yourself once the flower of youth has passed ...'

'Gone already,' Margaret interjected. Mitch reached over, smiled and took her hand.

'... we all are headed down Old Age Road, turning finally into Cemetery Street. There's nothing you can do to change that. But you can make it is pleasant as possible.

'We're like good products: we have a life cycle, and we must plan for our redundancy. Do you think the brains at Sony thought that the videotape format would last forever? No. As soon as they launched the product, they began planning what would happen when the product passed its use-by date. The company had to plan for the product's demise. Likewise us.

'The fact is that one day the workforce will throw you on a scrap heap. Thanks a lot. Bye-bye. Next please. When people tell me that's a horrible thing to say, my answer is just as horrible: "Grow up".

> Financial maturity means facing facts; your autumn is one of them.

'Don't let yourself be surprised by your autumn. It is the season when you have to be more independent than ever; a time when money has to keep coming your way without your doing anything. This is when self-generating wealth really matters.

'The thought of limping down the home straight for me is horrendous. I want to enjoy every bit of the autumn of my life. I want to savour every minute of this most peaceful season, not fret it away counting pennies and worrying about bailiffs.

> Plan to sail home smiling.

'Retirement planning is another subject in the broad curriculum of wealth education. It's something you have to study immediately, because it will influence many of the decisions you make.'

'Not more study!' Grace said.

'I'm afraid so. You'll have to put your head down and find a retirement plan. You'll need to look at ways of allowing your money to grow faster than in a savings account, you'll have to decide whether or not to seek the help of a retirement adviser, you'll have to examine benefit plans, profit-sharing plans and stock bonus plans. Then you'll have to get your head around all the special taxation rules concerning superannuation and capital gains.'

'Groan,' Grace said.

'I couldn't agree more. But it has to be done, so you might as well try to enjoy it. Retirement planning is a complicated subject, so we'd better move on before I lose you altogether.'

Rule 20: Plan, plan, plan.

'Planning for autumn is actually a sub-rule of a larger one that covers everything you do with money: Plan, plan, plan.'

'Like a good business,' Margaret said, mocking me.

'Exactly. And you don't need a thousand pages of information on how to plan. Here are the five essentials of good wealth creation, all beginning with my favourite word in the dictionary — "determine".' I handed around sheets of paper on which I had written the basics of good planning:

1   **Determine** the amount of wealth you need to consider yourself wealthy.
2   **Determin**e whether or not your present goals will get you to that level of wealth. If they won't, you'll have to stretch them.
3   **Determine** what level of financial literacy you need for each of your goals. Is it investment literacy, stockmarket knowledge, business planning? Draw up a skills path.
4   **Determine** where and how you will grow your money. If you don't want to do this, engage a financial planner.
5   **Be determined** to change your behaviour. Identify what you want to change about yourself, prepare yourself for permanent, zero-option change, then make an unbreakable promise to yourself to do it. Keep every promise, no matter what.

Rule 21: Persevere.

'The final rule I've selected for the rulebook of the rich is perhaps the most important: persevere. Do whatever it takes.

'Does anyone feel like giving up already?'

It had been a long session.

'It's only natural to feel that way. All successful people at some time in their lives have felt that they can't make it up that mountain; that they'd be better off just giving up. But they stick at it. The rich persevere.

'It's been said that you should never play a losing game. I say that you should never play a lost game, but I also say that you shouldn't give up until you are absolutely sure that you've lost the game.'

I paused and said quietly: 'And sometimes shit happens. Excuse my language.'

'How can you end on such a negative note?' Cathy asked.

'Because it's the truth, and the truth is neither negative nor positive — only your feelings about it are. Although it's been said many times before, most often by people far more qualified than I am, I will repeat it again now: "The truth will set you free." And that fills me with optimism.'

11. Dream and get real

This is the part I really love: learning how to dream with discipline.

It has become clear to me over the years that the rich dream differently from the not-so-rich. People living in the Rich Matrix create their dreams in precise detail and then start to live as if the dreams were already happening. People in the Bitch Matrix, on the other hand, have wild, imprecise fantasies. No wonder they bitch about their dreams never becoming reality.

There are dreams and there are fantasies. Dreams, properly dreamed, can become a blueprint for action. Fantasies, however, generally never amount to much more than wishful thinking.

> Distinguish between dreams and fantasies.

It's easy to wax lyrical about dreams. Eleanor Roosevelt, for instance, once said that the future belongs to those who believe in the beauty of their dreams. Walt Disney is famously quoted as saying that if you can dream it, you can do it. As inspirational as these statements sound, they don't really mean much. Dreaming with your eyes open, dreaming with discipline, however, makes a lot of sense.

> A dream is a possibility with a deadline.

I define a life-dream as "a real possibility with a deadline". In fact, I believe you run a life-dream the way you run a manufacturing business: you conceive a product, produce it, package it and then put it out into the marketplace. And you do it all according to a plan.

In the business of dreaming, you get your imagined self to work with your authentic self.

When we talk about dreams and reality we are dealing with two different, though not distinct, selves: the authentic self and the imagined self. I think of these selves in very simple terms: the authentic self is who you are, and the imagined self is who you want to be. Both are based on instinctive self-knowledge. Most sane people can tell the difference between the two, but few actually know how to get them to work together towards the same goal.

Everyone has his or her own life-dream. The challenge is to give it shape and substance. People often tell me they dream of being rich, but when I ask them to describe their one big dream, they are at a loss to furnish their life-dream with any precise financial details. It's all misty and fleeting. It's like manufacturing a product without knowing its size, its shape or even its usefulness. Such dreams won't do.

I have always found it challenging to get people to think of dreams and reality as partners, or the authentic and the imagined self as a unit. I am convinced, however, that it is only once you learn how to dream with your eyes open, how to add real detail to a life-dream, especially one concerned with wealth, that the exciting process of transforming the imagined into the real can begin.

> Your life-dream is anchored in reality.

I started this session by attempting some stirring, lyrical comments about dreams before I hit them with my no-nonsense version. I read deliberately from notes, as dramatically as I could.

> Fantasies make you feel good, but dreams with a deadline make you money.

'Dreams make people and their lives. They can also unmake both. For beyond the confines of rational behaviour, deep in the recesses of the unfettered mind, there's a great psychochemical laboratory where we're busy creating — or destroying — ourselves. This is the land of dreams, the home of volition, originality, creativity, passion and personal power. This is the deepest level at which you operate, where values, drivers, ideas, beliefs, passions are at their most combustible. It's here that the extraordinary self is conceived. Imagine a life without dreams, without those thousands of fantasies that enrich your waking, half-waking, sleeping and half-sleeping life. Deprived of them, life would be no more than a treadmill of dullness, a lot of expended energy getting nowhere.'

I paused.

'Blah, blah, blah, blah.'

The class was startled.

'It's all nice. It's probably all true, but it's air,' I said, tossing my notes onto the table.

'Toney, not again!' Margaret said.

'Do you want to feel good or make money?' I asked. 'Fantasies will make you feel good. But dreams with a deadline will make you money.

'I will admit that fantasies serve their purpose because they make life more bearable by allowing us moments of escape. Indeed without them, life would lose much of its colour. But the life-dream we are going to focus on is different. It's a life-dream with purpose, power and precision. In fact, we are about to learn about the business of dreaming.'

'The business of dreaming? Yuk!' Margaret said with a laugh in her voice.

'OK. The business of dreaming is not the most poetic of ideas, but who said making money was poetic? There's no poetry in a balance sheet and there's certainly no poetry in poverty. Besides, the business of dreaming is actually not as banal as it sounds. Anthropologists have written about Indian tribes who actually teach their children not only to dream deliberately but also to take control of their dreams by going in and out of them at will. That's the sort of dream hatched in the Rich Matrix.

'So welcome to our second-last session: Boot Camp for Dreamers.'

'Go get 'em, Toney!' Mitch said. It was unusual for gentle Mitch to be so spontaneous.

'We'll start by looking at the constituents of a managed life-dream.

A well-managed life-dream starts with a picture.

'The most important aspect of a well-run life-dream is that it is a picture. It's not a feeling, a yearning or a mood; it's a picture. My old friend Aristotle even went so far as to say that you cannot think without a picture.'

'Wait a minute, Toney,' Cathy said. 'You can dream of being in love without actually seeing the person you want to be in love with.'

'And you can dream of being rich without actually seeing just how rich,' Grace added.

'But that's not dreaming; it's fantasising. If you can't picture it, it's just wishful thinking.'

I turned to the whiteboard and wrote:

SEEING IS BELIEVING.

'OK,' I said. 'No points for originality. But look at the phrase, because my guess is that you've never really thought about its implications before. There's more wisdom in this phrase than in the entire literature of personal development. If you see something, you can believe it, and if you can believe it, it's real — at least to you. In fact, reality is described and understood by the pictures in our heads.

'Let's take a simple example. Imagine you're on a diet.'

'He's picking on Grace again,' Grace said to the rest of the class.

'Sorry, Grace,' I said. 'But being on a diet is no different from being on a budget. Tell us, then, what is Grace's downfall on a diet?'

'Chocolate.'

'Any sort of chocolate?'

'No. Her favourite brands.'

'You see, when Grace gets an uncontrollable urge for chocolate, it's not for generic chocolate, but for a real piece of chocolate, her favourite brand, just waiting for her to come and get it. I'm sure she could describe the wrapping, the text on the wrapping, the size, the price, even most of the ingredients of her favourite chocolate.'

Your desires proceed from mental pictures.

'Sure can,' Grace said. 'In fact, Toney, you should never have mentioned it.'

'See how the picture takes over. When it really comes into focus, it's good-bye diet.'

I tried another approach.

'What's on the two sides of a $100 bill?' I asked.

There was a general shrugging of shoulders.

'You all want to be rich, you want money to be part of your life-dream, and you can't even describe what a $100 bill looks like! Money is going to be a main part of your dream and you don't even know what it looks like! How could something so vague have any power in your life?

'In other words, for your single life-dream to have any power, it has to be clear in all its details. Not a thousand words, but a picture.'

'But what if you don't have a single life-dream?' Phil asked.

'Then it's time to get one,' I said. 'It's time to go looking for the one all-important dream that inspires you, the one life-changing conduit between the unconscious and conscious world — between who you are and who you want to be.

'You are therefore going to learn how to build — to manufacture — an authentic life-dream and how to place yourself as a wealthy person inside that dream.

'But you all must promise me one thing.' I paused and wrote on the whiteboard:

DREAM ONE DREAM WELL: YOUR LIFE-DREAM.

'This is the secret of a disciplined life-dream. You can change the details of your life-dream, but for the rest of your life it must remain basically the same.'

'What's the point of that, Toney?' Andy asked.

'Remember what we said about options, contingencies, alternatives?' I asked.

'They weaken commitment,' Andy replied.

'Right. You can't stick with your dream if it keeps changing. On the other hand, if it keeps coming more and more into focus, getting clearer and clearer, you will find that it also becomes more and more real.'

'Are you asking us then to commit to a dream?' Margaret asked.

'Like an unbreakable promise, like a change program, like a new habit. If you don't commit, it's just playing games.'

> Dreaming a life-dream is a serious business, it's for life.

I said nothing for almost a minute, wanting the class to understand that the business of dreaming was serious.

'This is not a feel-good session; dreaming is a serious business.'

I stared straight at them. 'Dreaming is a serious business,' I repeated.

There was no way to know whether or not they were ready to take me at my word, so I had to continue.

'OK. Let's go to the factory and begin to manufacture your dream.

'First, your vision, your picture, needs a canvas. Imagine a canvas in front of you. What is it like right now?'

> Start with a blank canvas.

'Don't we have to close our eyes? What about some music?' Grace asked.

I sighed, half exasperated. It's difficult to break through long-held beliefs.

'Sorry, none of that. No music or soft cushions. We're dreaming with our eyes open. It's going to take some practice, but your life-dream has to be so strong that you can picture it any time — with your eyes open. Don't worry. If

> Your life-dream is something you can always picture — anywhere, any time.

you concentrate long and hard enough, a blank canvas will come into focus.'

I could see the class straining to see.

'Where has Cathy put her canvas?' I asked.

'On her bedroom wall,' she said. 'It's huge and it's got absolutely nothing on it at the moment.'

'Andy's is on an easel in the living room.'

'Margaret's is in an artist's sketch book.'

'Phil prefers to sculpt his dream. There's a massive slab of clay in his back room.' Trust Phil to come up with something different.

'Good, everyone. Now don't change the place you put it. Not yet, anyway. That's the secret to good dreaming; it has to be certain. Just as things in the real world don't move unless you move them, so your canvas shouldn't move until you move it. Whatever you do, don't let it move without your permission.'

'It's definitely there,' Andy said, sounding slightly surprised.

Assume absolute authority over your life-dream.

'Now the next element of a well-planned life-dream is authority. Who's the boss?'

'We are,' Grace said.

'Exactly. Artists who put paint to canvas — or hands to clay — have absolute authority over their work. They can view their work from many angles and change it at any time, adding new features, new colours. For professional artists, a work is never released to the world until they decide it's right, it's finished. Until they put their brushes down.

'You have the same authority over your own canvas as an artist. You can zoom in, zoom out, add and subtract detail, until you're finally ready to let it go.

'This canvas or slab of clay is your imagined self.

You hold the editing controls of your life-dream.

But we're not going to think of the imagined self in the usual way of being infinitely flexible, undefined in size and shape, without fixed dimensions, boundaries or colour. No. You can't do anything with that sort of picture. Your life-dream, your imagined self, is subject to your authority. It can grow, shrink, overwhelm you or underwhelm you, but only if you let it. Only you can paint out the dark shadows, add light, capture stillness or create motion. Only you can erase the meaningless and the superfluous. The editing controls are in your hands. You're in charge.

Take charge of your life-dream.

'Taking control of your life has been the one great recurrent theme of the Rich Matrix. You control your choice, you control your passions, and you control your beliefs.

You can also control your imagined self. Take charge of your life-dream in your own way.

'Now let's put something on the canvas. You have already decided on the theme; it's written on your postcard to yourself. You now have to turn what you *really, really* want into pictures. Don't rush. Just take one picture and begin to paint it on the canvas. It can be anything consistent with what you really, really want. Just one thing. A house, a yacht, a CD collection, a size 10 dress, whatever.'

'Grace is having a hard time trying to see anything but a blank canvas.'

> Dream blindness is only temporary.

'Grace might think she can't see it very clearly at the moment, that there are no recognisable shapes making much sense. But it's there. All she has to do is learn to see again.

'Grace might in fact be suffering from temporary dream blindness, like the vast majority of people who haven't learned how to see their waking dreams clearly.

'Temporary dream-blindness can be caused by many things. Most of them have to do with the approach you take to this kind of dreaming; generally, the issue is beliefs that you've always held about your own inadequacy. You might, for example, feel that you have no control over your destiny, so you suspect that the whole exercise is pointless. Maybe you don't have confidence in your ability to live out your dream. Perhaps you believe that a passionate, compelling vision isn't meant for you; that you'll fail, or have to give more than you're capable of, or that it's too late for you. Or you believe that life is about compromise, about accepting what you have. These limiting beliefs, one on top of the other, can prevent you from seeing.

'If you can find out what's stopping your dream from emerging, you can learn to dream again.'

> Children dream the impossible; adults dream the possible.

'It feels so childish,' Mitch said.

'But wouldn't it be great to have the same childlike faith you once had? To be entranced and excited by what you truly want yourself to be? There is a difference, though, between the dreams of a child and your life-dream: your life-dream is possible. And if it's possible, it's also believable. So, dreamers, dream the possible.'

Dream and get real.

'Andy,' I asked. 'What do you see?'

'A house with a beach front,' he answered.

'Are you in the dream?'

'Of course.'

'Then get out of it immediately. You're in a half-built world. You'll get lost. Step out of it now!' I almost shouted.

'OK. OK,' he said, sounding repentant.

'What's the house like?'

'It's something from a movie. Lots of tall glass windows. A huge veranda. Deckchairs.'

'How many deckchairs are there, and what colour are they? Be careful when you answer, because you are choosing something that is going to be real. One day you will buy these deckchairs. So be careful. I repeat: be careful.'

'You're bonkers,' Margaret said.

'No, Margaret, not bonkers, just blinkers. What's the point of a life-dream that is not going to become real?'

Margaret looked down. I hoped I wasn't sounding too confrontational, but I had the hammer of reality in my hand and I was going to nail all these dreams to the spot, come what may.

'Margaret. What's the point of dreaming if it is not going to become real?' I repeated.

Margaret looked at me and softly admitted, 'I've never thought of it that way before.'

We smiled at each other.

'So, dreamers, of all the sessions we've had together, this is probably the most serious. This is where you leave the Bitch Matrix and cross over to the other side. This is where you wake from being the victim of your dream to being the master. And here's the best piece of advice I can give you: dream and get real.

'So Andy, tell me about those chairs.'

'There are two blue-and-white striped canvas deckchairs, with a small wicker table between them.'

'What's on the table?'

'Two long-stemmed glasses of something. A book.'

'Is the book open or closed?'

'Closed.'

'What's the title of the book?'

Andy shook his head.

'You may all think this detail is silly. That's because you haven't as yet experienced the power of detail. If Andy commits to this dream, if it's what he *really, really* wants, and he keeps adding detail to it every day, I'd bet my last dollar that sooner or later he will be sitting there.'

'This is all a bit too weird,' Margaret said.

It was proving difficult to win Margaret over.

'Which means Margaret is ready for the business side of this dream. What does Andy have to do to make his dream come true?'

'He has to find the money to buy the house,' Margaret said.

'Exactly. Just as someone with a product on the drawing board has to go looking for a venture capitalist or scrounge around for the money to manufacture the product themselves, Andy's dream needs financing. And he has to know exactly how much money he needs in order to make it work. So what do you think Andy should do?'

'Put a price on his house,' Mitch said.

'Yes. He has to start researching how much he needs to buy that house. In terms of the business of dreaming, he has to take the design of the product into the financing stage. If I were Andy, I would start my research immediately. Find the location, compare prices, look for one similar to your dreams and put a price tag to it. Even look at the price of those two blue-and-white striped deckchairs.'

Pennies dropped everywhere. I could see from the looks on their faces, even Margaret's, that this was making sense.

'The first step, then, is to start filling in the details of your big picture. It doesn't matter what it looks like. No one can see it but you, so no one can judge it, call it unrealistic or foolish. It's completely private. Dream it in front of you, as if it were forming right there before your eyes, at an arm's length, taking shape as you let your desires take over the brush. At the moment, keep it away from you, because at this point you must dream it outside yourself.

'In this session you won't be able to do much more than just begin your dream, so just have your canvas in place and a few scratches on it.

'The next step is like what happens in all manufacturing: it is a control process.

| *Authenticate your life-dream.* |

'You have to anchor your life-dream in authenticity. Turn on your authenticity filter; is your life-dream related to what you love doing and what you do best?

'It's a gut feeling. If it feels right, it is right. You've found an authentic storyboard for your own life. But if it feels wrong, if something doesn't quite fit, apply the alignment test. Is what you've chosen to include in your dream your choice or someone else's? Is it consistent with your sense of self? Does it ring true with your passions and values? Does it inspire optimism, rational or not?

'There are many questions you can ask yourself to authenticate your dream. What do you *really, really* want in your life in terms of people and things? What do you want to own? What sort of people do you want to be surrounded by? What do you want to experience? And what legacy do you want to leave behind?

'Remember that at this stage you're visualising, so avoid trying to see vague emotions such as joy, love and success.'

I then turned and wrote:

DREAM PEOPLE,
PLACES AND THINGS.

'That is not as materialistic as it sounds. People, places and things reflect your choices; they are the outward signs of an inward you. They provide the substance of your life-dream, anchoring it in reality. Having only a vague notion of what you want is like saying you're going on a journey to somewhere with someone. If your destination is not a definite place in time and space, you'll never get there, because you can't plan a trip to somewhere, with someone.

'The journey of your life is made up of specific sights and sounds. It's not just an idea. Like you, it's a world made up of molecules. The substance of your life therefore has a definite landscape; it's composed of the things you have chosen to possess, the people you have chosen to be with and the place you have chosen to be in. So make your dream as substantial as possible.'

'Isn't it easy to forget a life-dream?' Mitch asked.

'That's a good question, Mitch, and

Record your life-dream.

it brings us to the next task for the disciplined dreamer. When you leave tonight you have to begin to record this dream. Write it down. Paint it. Sculpt it. Weave it. Anything. Just turn the picture in your head into a real picture.

'Like everything else in this course, this is not a game. Recording your life-dream is a serious process, and you need to make it a high priority.

'One method many people use is to build up a montage from clippings in magazines or photos — whatever can help you visualise the people and things that reflect your choices, your desires, your needs and your responsibilities. And remember, choose carefully, because this life-dream, including your record of it, will be with you forever.

'I repeat: you must record it. If it's not recorded you'll lose it, because it won't be properly externalised, named, or given a shape you recognise, and it will therefore have little power. This is really important. Don't let the big picture slip away.

Enter your life-dream.

'The next step is to enter your life-dream. Don't rush to do this. You shouldn't put yourself into your life-dream until you know all its physical details. You need to know the place and the things in your life-dream before you move into it with your suitcase of feelings. It may be months before you're ready to enter your life-dream. Resist the temptation as long as you can.

'When you are ready to connect emotionally with it, you must feel it like you've never felt anything before. You must love your life-dream, possess it with all the madness of a jealous lover. Forget about being reasonable. Stepping into a waking life-dream is not normal behaviour.

People, places and things in your life-dream will turn up.

'By the time you're ready to step into your life-dream, you'll start to notice that certain things in your dream are already appearing in your daily life. You'll recognise them immediately. In fact, I have known people to be almost bowled over with amazement when things from their dreams — particularly if they don't remember seeing pictures of them before — come into their field of vision. It gives you an eerie sense of *déjà-vu*. I have no convincing explanation for this phenomenon. Some say it's the mind in filter mode, programmed to seek out what we've been feeding it as we construct our dreams. That seems plausible. Whatever the reason, it happens. One day Andy will actually see those blue-and-white striped deckchairs and the two long-stemmed glasses, and he will even recognise the book, provided he *manages* his life-dream.

'When you're ready to step into your life-dream, step in as the boss. Be the managing director. Be responsible for everything.

'The production line is where you'll need your best project management skills. After all, a dream with a deadline is a project. Andy, when will your house by the sea be ready?'

'Ten years,' he said.

'That's a sensible answer, and let's assume it's an informed guess. That means that as a good project manager you will draw up a ten-year plan, assign resources, set deadlines, track progress, manage cash-flow and keep on budget. This is what is meant by planned, disciplined dreaming, and it works.'

'So what's the difference between a dream and an actual business?' Andy asked.

'Nothing, really. You've even got shareholders in your dream, people you are responsible to — your family, for instance.'

I moved on to the next step.

'Not only do you have to picture

> Bring your life-dream to life.

your dream in vivid detail and then take control of it; you also have to bring it to life. You must speak, live and breathe as if your life-dream is already taking place.

'So start talking about your life-dream as if it was already happening, in all its vivid detail. Andy, for instance, is not going to save in order to be just a house-owner; he is going to work towards owning the particular house of his dreams, and he's going to start talking about it from today, even if he has only $10 to his name.

'It's an old trick that successful people use all the time. They actually get their unconscious mind to persuade their conscious, rational self that their dream has already materialised, which of course brings it closer to happening.

'I know one ex-bitcher who used to tell people she was happy with the way her finances were going and was planning a holiday in Europe. She studied her itinerary long before she had enough money to pay for her holiday. She wasn't lying; she was bringing her vision into the real world, making it happen in the realm of possibility, so that it would happen in the realm of probability and then in the world of actuality. In other words, she released her dream.

'Now we come to the final step.

Release your life-dream.

'You have to release your life-dream in order to make it happen. There are forces out there that we can't quite explain; dimensions and energies outside ourselves. You must hand over your life-dream to those forces. Don't ask me what they are — we are largely guessing when we start naming the unknown and the unknowable — but they certainly do exist.

'Releasing your life-dream is similar to the concept of attracting success. It's a way of having good things come to you instead of always chasing them. It's the key to unlocking synchronicity; the meaningful coincidence that happens when you have a desire for something and that something appears within minutes, hours or days.

'Synchronicity is part of the magical web of life that connects everything; it therefore beggars any rational explanation. You're thinking about a friend and that person calls you on the phone. You're looking for a perfect quote for your speech and a book falls open at the page with your perfect quote. You need someone with specific talents and you engage in conversation with a complete stranger who turns out to have exactly those talents.

'Releasing your life-dream means sending it out into the realm of connected possibilities where what you dream and what happens become synchronous.

'I think we will end this session with a mnemonic to help you remember the life-dreamer's discipline. Here it goes:

D is for dreaming people, places and things.
R is for recording your life-dream.
E is for entering it,
A is for authenticating it,
M is for managing it,
E is for enlivening it by stepping right into it, and
R is for releasing it.'

12. Brand new chapters

On the morning of our last session I got up early and went jogging.

While they were probably putting the final touches to their commitment speeches, I spent the day reviewing my teaching and wondering about what part of it would live on in their memories now that the course had finished. What would stand the test of time? What would have a lifetime impact?

I knew what I wanted them to take away with them. The only thing that mattered was to be true to your own word. The only way to become rich, thin, learned, athletic, respected, first, fast, powerful, famous, whatever ... was to do what you say you're going to do. That's what it's all about. So simple, yet so difficult.

In fact, the message had already stood the test of time. My observations, my particular approach to the problem of personal excellence, my slivers of advice on how to build wealth, had all been restatements of one piece of wisdom that has been repeated throughout recorded history, a piece of wisdom that writers, scholars, philosophers, priests and laity, executives and janitors, mums and dads have kept coming back to for hundreds of years:

To thine own self be true.

Or as I had phrased it, much less poetically, 'Keep the promises you make to yourself.'

Why has this lesson, which teaches us the only sure and sensible way to achieve success and happiness, been so hard to learn?

I sat down on the beach, just as the sun was strong enough to begin warming the sand, and tried to order my thoughts.

I had tried to be honest with these seven people. Since I move in a circle of successful people, and they don't, all I had hoped to do was give them the benefit of my experience, pass on what successful people had taught me.

I wondered how their preparation was going. Had they been able to write the beginning of a new story? What would they say? Going public with a commitment to change is not easy.

Who would they invite to witness this commitment, I wondered. Mitch and Margaret seemed to live in a world of their own, and I couldn't imagine them having many close friends. Phil had said he was happiest alone, so he was likely to come alone. What about Andy? He had never mentioned a wife or partner, so who would he bring? Would Grace's boyfriend be able to cope? What would Cathy, who had seemed to lose interest in the last few lessons, say in her speech?

Take a bit of your own medicine, doctor, I said to myself. *I won't worry about any of this until 4.30pm this afternoon*. I laughed at myself and headed home.

I arrived at the restaurant early. We had reserved the whole restaurant in order to guarantee our privacy. Cathy, who had volunteered to organise the night, was there to meet me.

'Table for thirty-eight, sir?' she said as she approached me.

'My God!' I said. 'Has Grace invited the whole street?'

'No. The biggest group is for Phil.'

What Phil hadn't told me was that he played football. He therefore thought it only natural to invite his whole team.

'And he's bringing his partner,' Cathy added.

'He never told me he had a girlfriend,' I said.

'He doesn't. His partner's a he. Apparently, they used to play football together.'

It was to be a night of surprises.

Within half an hour of everyone arriving, the mood turned electric. Chairs were claimed, introductions were made, corks popped and food was served. I can't remember who was who among the friends and family, except for a few who stood out: Grace's partner, Michael, because he was a living tableau of tattoos, Andy's girlfriend, Christina, because she was stunningly beautiful, and Phil's partner, Trent, because he was in a wheelchair.

Finally, the waiter signalled that coffee was about to be served. It was my cue to begin.

'Welcome, everyone, to a very special day in our lives. I presume you all know what this is about, so I will only say a few words and then hand over the floor to our graduates.

'The reason you are here is because you are an important part of their world. They want to enrol you in their future, because without your support the permanent changes that they will make in their lives, or have already made, will fizzle out.

'Each of the six course participants will be reading a commitment speech. This is a public declaration of the change they seek in their lives and their commitment to bring about that change. Such a change is both profound and permanent. That has been the theme of the three months we have spent together.

'You have probably heard them talk about promise-making and maybe even *metanoia* — the complete, radical conversion to a new way of living. Tonight they will make a single promise — that they will live by the promises they make to themselves — and begin a new chapter in their lives. We have called this the Empowering Promise.

'"What's the big deal?" you may ask. Well it may sound simple, but as they will tell you, it's very serious. They are saying that any serious promise they make to themselves cannot be broken. No matter what.

'The power by which they seek to achieve more in their lives is based on the unbreakable promise. If a promise has been made carefully, solemnly and authentically, it remains forever. There's no contingency planning, no sunset clause, for these kinds of promises. They are as serious as a person's wedding vows.

'That's where you all come in.

'Their promises may disrupt the world you share with them. Your relationship with them may change — for better or worse. You therefore need to be prepared for the changes ahead.

'I know it sounds as if we're running some sort of secret society here. But none of us is wearing robes or chanting from mystical texts. I've spent weeks getting rid of all the gobbledegook you read about personal power. So you'll find no codes or sacred handshakes, no miracles. Not even a good fire-walk.

'We have only one rule: *To thine own self be true*. It is the ultimate rule of self-mastery, and it means we need no masters but ourselves, no code of conduct beyond those six words, no authority but our own word.

'So tonight is their night. I am as anxious as you are to know what they will say, but in the end it doesn't really matter, as long as it's true. For the truth will set them free.'

Margaret

'I know most of you wonder why someone like me hasn't made it. I look and sound like I have all the attributes of a successful person — I am tough, determined and resourceful. Well, that's what I look and sound like, but the truth is otherwise. I have been paralysed for years.

'Ten years ago, when I was out on holiday in Australia, I met Mitch. He was so full of fun and we shared so many dreams that I thought I was in for a life of endless adventure. I said goodbye to my home in Chelsea, London, my nice British middle-class life, packed my bags, married Mitch and moved to Australia. I was 25 years old. I was in love with the man and the country, both full of possibility.

'Mitch was working for an engineering firm at the time. Since I was trained to teach mathematics, I took a job in a high school. I hated it. Something was not right. I couldn't stand the daily fight with the kids, the principal's ego and the pushy parents. I didn't even know why I was teaching maths. I was not particularly gifted, and I clearly wasn't an inspiring teacher. The students didn't like me as a maths teacher, the staff didn't like me, and I liked neither students nor staff. But more significantly, I didn't like myself, particularly as a maths teacher. After three years of this, I couldn't take it any longer. I resigned, believing that I would be able to do something else. Up till now, I haven't found that something else.

'Four years into our marriage, I was told that I could never have any children. The news fell on me like a load of bricks. I remember the day in the doctor's surgery when the verdict was delivered as clearly as if it was this morning. I remember it because it seems that from that moment my whole life started to go downhill. There were alternatives, I know, but I wouldn't listen. I couldn't shake free of the knowledge that I was barren, from the belief that somehow I wasn't whole. I felt so cheated, so let down by life, robbed of a precious part of being a woman.

'It was two years later — two years of unemployment and feeling sorry for myself — when lightning struck a second time. Mitch was forced to resign from his engineering job because some political bigwig made a mistake and needed a scapegoat.

'Six months later, lightning struck a third time. Mitch's twin brother died and he turned to me for support, which I wasn't able to give. But I will let him tell you his story. It wasn't enough that my life was rolling downhill; now we were tumbling down together.

'We had to give up our dream of owning our home, so we moved into rented accommodation and spent the next three years arguing about money. Our marriage was on the point of collapse. I had changed, Mitch had changed, and it was only by some miracle that we stayed together. Of course it was all his fault.

'I turned completely anti-social and buried myself in my painting. I am not a good artist — I know this now — but it was the one thing that gave me an escape. At least it wasn't drink or drugs. I did some maths tutoring to pay for my art supplies, and left Mitch with the task of finding a household income.

'When I started to feel guilty that I wasn't helping to pay my way, I took a few of my best pieces to a local art dealer in the hope that they might bring us some much-needed income until Mitch found his way out of his own darkness.

'The dealer's judgement burned a hole in my head. "You haven't got what it takes," he said. The words reverberated for hours. I lost control that night, got drunk, lit a fire in the backyard and threw everything I had ever painted into it. Some nice neighbour rang the fire brigade and I got into terrible trouble. At the time, it didn't matter. I thought it was the ultimate liberation.

'The problem was that the next morning I woke up and nothing had changed.

'I have spent the last few years dreaming of getting on a plane, going back to London and picking up the pieces of my old life. I have such fond memories of the comfortable life I lived there, albeit at the expense of my family. But I can't go back. I have been pretending, for the sake of my own self-esteem, that everything has been going all right. I have even been lying to my father in our weekly conversations over the last few years — my mother died when I was two — making up excuses for why we couldn't get over to visit.

'When Toney talked about doing the one thing that was truly me, I knew what it was: it had to have something to do with art. So it just wasn't fair. Nature was not able to provide me with the talent to do the one thing that truly inspired me. It was so cruel.

'I know that painting is right for me. It's the time I feel in the zone. I can paint for hours, lose myself in colours and images.

'I think the most powerful words I heard in this course were "What you love doing is what you do best." Well I love painting, but obviously it is not what I do best.

'As I told the class, I am the world's best shopper. I can find anything, anywhere, anytime. Then it dawned on me. I should combine the two.

'You all know how cynical I am. I don't listen to New Age talk, so when Toney mentioned synchronicity, I nearly threw up.

'Now I love that word. It has both a scientific and a magical ring to it.

'Exactly two weeks ago, I was in a gallery in Sydney, and started talking to a stranger I was sharing a table with in a nearby café. She told me how she made money as an art dealer. The conversation lasted over three hours; it was a marathon question and answer session. She worked on a commission basis and made her money by spotting talent and offering to sell it. Most of it privately. She had made enough money to start investing in art herself.

'At last I had found what I *really, really* wanted to do.

'I have already promised myself that I will do it, whatever the effort. I am taking this promise-making very seriously, because I think Toney is right. The only way I can get out of the ill-defined world I live in is to bring a bit of uncompromising discipline into it.

'I also understand what Toney means about the what ifs and contingency thinking in decision-making. Oh, I understand it all too well. Alternatives have eaten away at all my plans like hordes of voracious termites.

'I also took on board what he said about differentiating oneself and about doing something once and selling it many times. For me this means that I have to set up a dealership that will run itself. In other words, one in which both the buyer and the seller come to me. Since conceiving it this way, the ideas have come flooding in.

'I have given myself a year. When that postcard arrives, with my promise on it, I am absolutely sure I will be able to say to myself that I have kept this promise.

'If I can keep this one promise, if this kept promise can put me back into the driver's seat of my own life, who knows how far I will go? I might even stop being the world's biggest bitch!

'Maybe Toney is right. With this sort of either/or approach to getting things done in life, maybe we can all be unstoppable.'

Mitch

'Marg has already mentioned the hardest blow life has dealt me so far: the death of my twin brother. It was much harder than becoming redundant at the age of 32.

'It's very difficult to tell people what being a twin is like, but most of the weird stuff they say about twins is true.

'Josh and I loved being identical twins. We were the two most inseparable, closest human beings you could ever meet. We both married English women — we're suckers for punishment — we were both engineers, and yes, sometimes we bought the same clothes without the other knowing.

'Like Marg, I am not a spiritual person, but I still talk to Josh. He might not be around physically, but he's still part of me. It's my way of praying, I suppose. When Marg gets into one of her moods, I drive down to the beach where he drowned and the two of us spend a few hours bitching about our wives.

'Josh made me laugh. Like Marg did before the troubles started. So when Josh died, the last bit of laughter in my life went with him.

'My escape from all this was a dangerous one. I'm not ashamed to tell you, because I think you're all intelligent enough to realise that addictions are not really very different from other sicknesses for which no one is expected to feel guilty.

'I turned to gambling. Odd, isn't it, that gambling takes hold of people who don't have the money to gamble? I don't know how it started, but for almost a whole year I played the poker machines night after night.

'I lost what remained of our savings and was on the verge of losing Margaret, the other great love of my life. It was the most stupid thing I have ever done. Sitting there every night of the week being hypnotised by a roll of silly pictures. Of course I almost always left with nothing, even on the odd nights when I'd hit a small jackpot.

'It was obvious that my life was not going to get better with a big win falling down from the sky. But I had lost the will to do anything to change the direction of my life. I was hoping for my circumstances to change without my doing anything. I was like the ball in Newton's first law — I was moving in a straight line at the same speed, and would continue to do so until a force was exerted to get me to change direction.

'When Toney talked about Newton's laws of change, as an engineer, he was speaking my language. I stopped thinking about all the reasons behind my addiction. I focused on cause and effect. I put money in a machine at ludicrous odds, I pressed a button and I lost it. It was as simple as that. Bitching about being a victim of circumstances had only muddied these very simple facts. I was feeding my self-pity with a silly story, when the facts of gambling were so clear. The truth — the facts without the story — had set me free.

'If I was going to change, I would have to make a promise to never put another cent into those stupid machines again. A promise for life. I think it was week four when I made that promise, when I finally got what was meant by an unbreakable promise. Now, you could put a gun to my head and I still wouldn't play a machine.

'I made the promise on my wedding ring. That's a serious thing to do, I know. But I have linked it to my vow to Margaret to stay with her, the most serious promise I have ever made. I don't know how we have managed to stay married, falling downwards like this together, but we have.

'The gambling bit, actually, was only a side issue. Over the last couple of months I have thought about the kind of power such promise-keeping could have. If it worked with gambling, which was probably only just a wayward phase in my life, anyway, why wouldn't it work with everything else?

'All the little sound bites Toney had given us began to make sense. Take control. Life is short. Time is a non-renewable resource. Do something. Think cause and effect. Zero options. Metanoia. Either/or.

'So I said to myself, *Right, that's enough. I am going to do something.*

'For a long time I have resisted going into private consultancy with someone I know. The other day I rang him. We're meeting next week. Even if nothing comes of it, it is a start. I have changed the direction of that damn ball. How simple was that?

'The best part occurred last week. Marg and I had been talking about our life-dreams. But we figured that it would be pretty stupid having different life-dreams, because we wanted to live in partnership. So we reasoned that if we could destroy our life-dream together, we could also build it together.

'Marg got out her paints, and together, with our eyes open, we dreamed. Naturally, we argued from the beginning. The first thing we agreed on was a dog. Now I know that sounds really silly, and all of you are probably dreaming of sweeping views and apartments and flashy cars, but Marg and I dreamed of a dog. Marg has already painted it. It's a black labrador.

'The next thing, of course, was a garden. You can't have a dog without space. But we didn't want just a garden; we both wanted a farm. Independently and naturally, our life-dreams crossed. It was only two days ago. I don't remember having had this much fun for years. I also don't remember being as close to Marg before.

'The farm took shape, and do you know what? It was Margaret's answer to her business idea — she was going to set up a permanent art farm. Artists in residence and all that. This was to be a place for buyers and artists to meet. It was perfect.

'I have no idea yet how we are going to do it. But it seems so perfect. So authentic, as Toney would say. And what's more, we will do it together.

'So far there's not much more in the picture than the labrador — we decided to call him after Neo in *The Matrix* – and a whole expanse of grass, but we've started to dream with our eyes open. We're going to run our dream like a business: cost it, plan for it, and devote resources to it.

'One more weird thing has happened. Marg told me this morning that she wanted to call the farm and her business after Josh. I had planned to suggest exactly the same thing tonight.

'Looks like we're really and truly in it together.

Andy

'I think I'd better start by introducing Christina to you. This gorgeous woman and I have only been dating for a month. I asked her here tonight because I thought that if we do start up a relationship, she might as well know me as I really am.

'Remember the other night when we all made fun of each other? We gave ourselves titles. There was Margaret the Queen of Bitches, Mitch the King of the Browbeaten, Grace the Lady of the Larder, Cathy the Crème in Your Coffee, and of course Phil the Philosopher. Remember how you couldn't come up with a name for me? Finally, smart Phil hit on it: Andy the Anonymous.

'And that's me. A nowhere man going nowhere.

'I'm a drifter. I even drifted into my present job because I couldn't think of anything better to do.

'I'm also glad my boss Leon is not here to witness this, because I have a confession to make. I lied about my qualifications and experience to get this job. I thought it didn't matter at the time because I was only going to use it as a stepping-stone to something else, but I still have no idea what that something is.

'Actually, I like being a salesman, even if it is just selling workflow applications. It's not very exciting stuff, but I get a real buzz about hitting those numbers. I think selling is second nature to me. I can phone anyone, anytime, and get them interested in a product. It's a real talent.

'I have been in this job now for five years. We're a small company and we will probably remain so, because Leon is not very keen to take risks. Both the company and I seemed doomed to anonymity.

'One of the best exercises of this course was the Bridget Jones Exercise. I suppose, like many of you, I have stopped and started things, been on the verge of making some changes and then pulled back. I never imagined myself as powerless, though. After all, you have to have a lot of confidence in yourself to be a salesman. But that's what would happen. When it came to myself, I lacked confidence. So did the one woman I loved. She turned me down, she said, because I was going nowhere.

'She even rang me from the bedroom of her new lover. Some bastard of a millionaire. They were getting ready to go on a skiing holiday to Whistler, Colorado. I couldn't afford to take her on the ferry to Manly, let alone halfway round the world. OK, you could say that she was nothing but a materialist and therefore it was best that she was gone. But that's not the point. The point was that she was right. I was a nobody.

'The sales confidence is only bravado. Underneath, there's this feeling of being so empty, so unimportant in the world, so anonymous.

'Remember when I had to play the unfaithful husband? Well, that hurt more than you can imagine, because when I finally stop being a lad — you know, "one of the boys" — I want to have a family. Lots of children. And give them the best of everything.

'Money has never interested me. Strange for a salesman, you could say, because a good salesman is driven by money. But for me it's different. I get my salary and my bonuses and blow the lot. Fun has always been my number one driver.

'I am only 28, but when I did the Bridget Jones exercise I was really shaken. In 20 years' time I saw myself doing the same thing. There was one slight change. I was a director of sales. But I had only one salesman underneath me. The worst part was that I think I saw myself as a bachelor.

'When Toney said that we are all characters in the story of our own making, I remember going home and wondering about my own story. What plot had I woven for myself? What script had I written? Could I change it?

'In my story I am Peter Pan. Never growing up. Good for a lark. No responsibilities, no ties, just out for a good time. Someone who just couldn't be bothered with all the effort it takes to do something extraordinary. My character didn't even believe he had something extraordinary to do.

'The story I had written for myself actually had no plot. As its central character, I was just going from scene to scene, heading nowhere. But try as I could, I had no idea what needed to be changed.

'No wonder I am scared about entering another relationship. Who wants to be with someone who's really not anyone?

'*Go somewhere, be someone*, I have kept saying to myself throughout this course. I have to go somewhere. Then Toney warned us about somewhere and someone.

Unless it's somewhere particular, it's nowhere; unless its someone definite, it's no one.

'So I thought, *Why not just dump the whole story and start again?* Why not treat my life as some sort of experimental drama I was bumbling around in, and step out and write an entirely new story? After all, the only reason I never grow up in my story is because I'm writing the damn thing. I could rewrite it and be a winner. But how?

'I decided to give promise-keeping a go.

'Instead of buying a commitment ring, I bought this earring I'm wearing tonight. It cost a lot more than I could afford, but I figured that it had to be special. When Toney talked about transferring power to a symbol of commitment, I reasoned that the best way to transfer power to a symbol was to begin to reverence it.

'I have a special box for it in my bedroom, you know, like an altar. Sounds psycho, I know, but something's happening. It's not turning gold and flying around the room or any of that stuff, and I haven't made any promises on it yet, because I haven't come up with a serious promise yet. But something is definitely happening. I have spent the last couple of weeks just looking at my earring, wearing it, feeling it. Acting a bit like Frodo in *The Lord of the Rings*. The difference is that this earring of mine is good. It will work for my good; it will give me access to whatever power I have inside me.

'Each time I touch it, I get a funny feeling. Toney called it anchoring — or something like that — externalising an inward reality.

'When I told a mate about this he thought I'd gone mad. "Too much clubbing has affected your brain," he told me. "Stop taking whatever you're taking, dude," he said.

'I don't understand what's happening. All I know is that I am beginning to feel a sense of power and it's exciting me, perhaps unnerving me. How weird is that? It sounds incredible, but I am really convinced that this little piece of jewellery is going to make me powerful. An unbreakable promise made on this earring has just got to happen, otherwise the earring is nothing and I am no one.

'Imagine it. Whatever I promise to do I will do.

'I don't have any great plans to build wealth. I'm just enthralled at the moment about the fact that personal power is possible.

'Last night I tried the Bridget Jones exercise at home, this time with my earring on. I took myself 10 years, 15 years and 20 years into the future, and I got a glimpse of something. I was going to some award ceremony — now you are probably going to think that my mate was right, I have done too much clubbing, but it's true. I walked into a room and there was a lot of applause. I have no idea what it was about.

'I don't know if I will make great wealth. I haven't been able to put the slightest outline of anything on my canvas yet. It's still completely blank. But I do know now that if I keep the promises I make to myself I will have power to do whatever I decide to put on that canvas.

'When I gave Toney my postcard, I thought he would fire me, because it simply said: "By January 31st 2006 I will know what I really, really want to do." He accepted it. He must have known it would take me that long.

'Tonight I have begun. I promise tonight, in front of you all, that any promise I make on this earring will be binding. I have tonight willingly become a slave to my own word.'

Phil

'There's a famous scene in *Whatever Happened to Baby Jane?* when Joan Crawford, playing the crippled Blanche in a wheelchair, turns to her nasty sister, played by her real-life enemy, Bette Davis, and says:

'"You wouldn't be able to do these awful things to me if I wasn't in this chair."

'"But ya are, Blanche, ya are in that chair!"

'Trent and I often laugh over that scene, but we reverse the roles. He says my wheelchair is my desk chair and I'm the one who's crippled.

'He's right, you know.

'Trent's quite well off, since he's built up a successful business online, so he could easily replace me with a nurse. But he won't, because he knows I need him far more than he needs me.

'In the five years since the accident, which we never talk about since he says it's just a badly written drama that bores him, I have never, ever, caught him feeling sorry for himself. Needless to say, he catches me at it almost every day.

'He'll throw something at me if I start holding him up as an example of courage and all that, so I have to get this over quickly. I asked him to come along tonight not only because we do almost everything together, but mainly because he's worth a thousand of Toney's lessons.

'Ladies and gentlemen, behold someone who always does what he says he will do.

'And I'd better change the subject now or I'll be out on the street tonight.

'One of the great things about being a cabbie is that you get to learn a lot, especially if you're a good listener. You can also make a fairly good living, if you're prepared to clock up the hours.

'As you know, I fancy myself as a writer. I have been writing stories for years. As yet I haven't had anything published. Basically, because I never finish anything I write. I once got to over 200 pages in a novel and just walked away from it.

'The difference between a writer and an author is that a writer writes, and an author sells. When Toney started talking about stepping aside and looking at your life without the emotion — the way a bank manager looks at your account, seeing figures, not vague shapes — I realised that I couldn't see my writing through the unemotional eyes of a publicist with a product to sell.

'Writing is what I love doing and it's what I do best. Selling myself is not something I do well at all. I can't do what Andy does. I couldn't sell a bottle of water in the desert. Even at a discount. The problem is that in my story — the real one of my life — the main character is so weak. He's always going in someone else's direction. When my fare says take me to so and so, that's what I do. If someone tells me I'm no good, I believe them. If someone asks me a favour, I generally do it. I have reached a point of chronic learned helplessness. I feel so disabled. And as Trent would put it, "But ya are, Phil, ya are."

'Every night after my shift I take the stories I've heard that day and weave them into my fiction. You wouldn't believe how open some people are when they're in the cab with you. You're like a priest in a confessional. And because they have limited time, if something is on their mind, they have to get it out in a hurry, so they usually stick to the essentials. It's like the proverbial salespitch-in-the-elevator. They've all got something to say: criminals, saints, idiots, geniuses, the broad-minded and the generous, the nasty and the bigoted, the broken-hearted and the star-struck. For source material it's a writer's dream, especially if you know what questions to ask.

'Trent loves my stories. He's often threatened to send them off to a publisher if I don't. So I keep them securely password-protected, because I'm just not ready for that sort of exposure.

'Why not? Why haven't I turned out a bestseller? Is it because I can't write? No, that's not it. Bestsellers don't need to know how to write well; they just need to know how to sell well.

'My postcard said, "By December 2006, I will have a book doing the rounds of the publishers and agents." Toney sent it back to me. He has seen how much I have written, so his instructions were simple and blunt: do it in half the time, or don't bother doing it. When Trent heard about it, he applauded.

'I remember getting really angry at Toney. *The little creep*, I thought. *How would he know what writing is like?* Of course there's a lot of pleasure in writing, but it's still one of the most painful and exhausting things you can do. And you're always comparing yourself with a famous writer, a teacher or a bestselling author. You wander in and out of self-doubt all the time, listening to the nasty editors in your head telling you it's rubbish. *Am I using too many adjectives? Is this character believable? Should I do some more research? Does it flow? Oh no, the structure's collapsed!* If you think writing is romantic, think again. It's much, much easier to drive a taxi.

'As far as budding writers go, I am privileged. I have a source of income that can support what I love doing and the greatest man alive as my partner, someone who'd support me whatever stupid things I do. But I had to answer the question: Do I *really, really* want to do more than just write for a hobby? Do I *really, really* want to be an author? To do whatever it takes? Which means facing rejection slips, selling myself, building a network, actually meeting with other writers.

'I decided — I have recorded it in my blog if you want to go online and read it — that yes, I *really, really* want to be an author more than anything else in the world.

'In my blog I have created a special section for my promise book. Toney is right. The only way for me to force myself to keep a promise is to make it public. I am too vain to let myself down in front of the whole world;

too fragile to have anyone mock me for not being true to myself.

'There are only three promises in my promise blog. The first is that every promise entered into my promise blog becomes a sacred, solemn vow that must be fulfilled at all costs. That's the Empowering Promise. The second promise is, of course, my postcard date.

'The third promise was the hardest one. I worked out how many words I could write in a night, or on one of my days off, and how many words I would need for my first novel — which is about a cabbie, of course. I wanted to add a promise to my blog that I would write so many words per day. I hesitated and thought, *No, writing is not like that.* A writer's not a machine. There are moods and all sorts of internal battles to fight.

'But there is another side to the writing game. Discipline. It pays to write a certain number of words every day, even if they're nonsense. So instead of staring at a blank page, you just write whatever comes into your head, freely, non-stop, without editing. Strangely enough, these are often your best words.

'I have therefore made a promise never to write less than 500 words a day until a publisher accepts my book. That's not many, and I usually write a lot more, so I was really surprised to learn how so few words could be such a bother. It doesn't matter how tired I am, what's on the television, who's coming to dinner, what Trent wants to do, etc. I have to get those 500 words done. I've only been doing it for two weeks, and I have already run into problems. But I have done it, am doing it, and will continue to do it until my book is on the bookshelf.

'I must. It's in my promise blog – which is, by the way, the best thing I have ever written.

'Just as importantly, I must, because if I don't, that pain-in-the-butt over there in the wheelchair might one day just get tired of having a loser hanging around. And then I would lose something I could never recover.'

Grace

'You all know two things about me: one, that I'm a hairdresser and, two, that I have a weight problem.

'I came on this course after I ran up the back of Toney's car. It was, by the way, his fault. When we got talking, he told me to come to the first session, even if I wasn't interested in making mountains of money. He said that the course was about getting what you wanted in life. So I turned up, and here's my story.

'I love being a hairdresser. I'm good at. I'm actually good enough to create a style and franchise it. The problem is that I don't *really, really* want to do it all my life. Opening my own salon would be fun and all that, but when Toney started talking about what I *really, really* wanted to be, what the one thing I wanted in my life was, it wasn't cutting hair.

'What I *really, really* want to be is a fitness instructor. Yep, the opposite of what I am now. I thought it was just a silly dream. Something to do with my obsession about losing weight. But then I asked myself, *Why not?* What is to stop me? I'm still young.

'It's Newton's Third Law, isn't it? "To every action there is an equal and opposite reaction." Just listen to me! Here I am quoting physics and I absolutely hated it at school!

'The Bridget Jones exercise was a terrible experience for me. I couldn't even see the original movie more than once, because she was exactly like me. Stuffing her face whenever she felt bad about herself. And the diets! Like her, I've done them all.

'My first step was to take hold of the facts. Do you know what I discovered? Other people have tried to cover up the facts as much as I have! When I go on about losing weight, they tell me it doesn't matter. They say that I'm a warm, happy person with so much to give. Michael's been giving me that line for years. "Pleasantly plump", he says. Bullshit. I'm fat, and I hate myself for being fat. I'm a size 18, for heaven's sake. That's more than plump, and it's far from pleasant.

'I once went to a psychologist to see if the problem was deeper than just being Miss Piggy. She managed to drag up so many things from my past that after every session I'd go home and attack my fridge like a real desperado.

'So I got on the scales, determined to take Toney's advice and just look at a number. No emotions. That's how much I weigh. Full stop. *Get over it, girl*, I kept saying, using one of his favourite expressions.

'So, here's what happened.

'I admitted what I am: I'm fat. Then I admitted what I *really, really* wanted to be: a fitness instructor.

'Yep. Why just drop down a size or two? Would that make me happy? For a little while, maybe, but then I would probably just put it all back on. What I wanted was another me. I wanted a complete makeover, but not just superficially. I wanted to feel good about myself. I wanted to be active again, go on the ski slopes, ride a pushbike, swim laps in a pool. That's what I *really, really* wanted more than anything in the world.

'I suppose it makes sense, doesn't it? When you don't like what you are, you want to be the opposite of it. The funny thing is that when I think about being a fitness instructor it feels so authentic; it's *so* me!

'And it's not like it's impossible. It's not like I'm asking myself to win the Nobel Prize or anything, is it?

'Now here comes the funny bit. When Toney got us started on our life-dream, I knew I had to be in the centre of it, but he told us we couldn't do that, not immediately anyway. That annoyed me, because my dream was not about people, places and things; it was about me. How could I dream this and not put myself dead smack in the middle?

'I found a solution. For the last two months or so, I have walked past this absolutely beautiful size 12 dress so many times that I could describe every fibre of it. So, I thought, while others are dreaming about things that will come their way, I will do it the other way around. I will put it in my way and then dream it.

'I bought the dress. It's waiting for me in my cupboard. You can't get a more definite part of a life-dream than that, can you?

'I have also learned that if I know what I *really, really* want in life, it can no longer be a part-time interest. Losing weight and taking up exercise — even beginning my instructor's course — will mean full-time commitment. It's not something I do for an evening or two; it's something I will do for the rest of my working life.

'I have already got some info on training courses, met an instructor and explained my dream to him. You know what he said? I wanted to shout it from the treetops. I couldn't believe it. He reached into his pocket and showed me a photograph of himself. My God, he was like a beach ball. He was twice my size!

'"Far fatter people have done this and succeeded." That's what he said! I can be a fitness instructor!

'I went back to my life-dream and I put in a treadmill and a set of free weights. And do you know what? They were mine. They belong in the gym that one day I will own.

'Lady Larder will have a gym instructor's certificate in 18 months. That's my promise. And she's going to take to fitness like a bird to the air. You'd better believe it, because this little bird does.'

Cathy

'I'm sorry to tell you, but I think I've failed the course. Well, not really failed, but I've realised that I don't *really, really* want to be wealthy.

'Oh it would be nice having lots of money. Don't get me wrong. But I have admitted that it takes too much commitment. As Toney says, it's not just a matter of thinking and growing rich, it's a matter of doing. And I have lots of other things I'd prefer to do.

'I have thought hard about this. I have a very simple desire in life: to be a mother. I know I can be a successful career woman and a good mother. Plenty of women do that. But it's not what I want. I simply want to find a lovely husband and be a full-time mother.

'All this talk about time and money management is just not me. It doesn't ring true for me. It's inauthentic. I am happy with very little and I have now made a profound decision: to live within those simple needs.

'In this sense, the course has been successful for me. I have determined what I truly want in life, and it's not a lot of money; it's enough money to pay the bills, keep independent, and provide what is necessary for my family.

'I am different from the rest of you. I don't think being able to send my children to private schools and buy them anything they want will make them happy or make me any more of a good mother.

'I work as a manager — waitress, really — in a busy café and I love my work. I love serving other people. I love their smiles. I even love their grumpy moods. Why should I go through the sweat and worry of owning a restaurant? Would it make me happier? No.

'At last I know. At last I have admitted it. The truth has set me free.

'And it feels great!

'When I left school, everyone thought I would do medicine or law, because I was a star pupil. But the only reason I was good at school was because I enjoyed it. I never had any intention of giving myself over to a career, because I knew I wouldn't enjoy it. I will fulfil myself as a full-time mother. This is what I *really, really* want. I am absolutely 100 per cent certain of this.

'Maybe I'm old-fashioned, a dinosaur. But I'm finally able to be completely honest.

'I want ordinary happiness, and I want to be proud of that choice. I will try to be an extraordinary mother, but not out of personal ambition or any great desire for success. I will do it for a much more selfish reason: giving to others makes me happy. I want only the return that comes from caring.

'Some of us were born to be carers — the hewers of wood and carriers of water. We can't all be masters. We can't all be leaders and pioneers. That wouldn't make any sense.

'I am choosing a different path from the rest of you, because what I seek in my life is not wealth; it is love. It is only in love that I will be really true to myself.

'By the way, you might be wondering what was on my postcard. Well it's really ordinary, but it's a promise I know I can keep: I promise to host our reunion, a year from now.'

I was so happy to hear Cathy's speech. The course could not have ended on a better note. Getting rich is a choice. She had understood that perfectly and had made her choice. More importantly, she had the courage to be true to herself. It was no wonder the entire crowd stood up and applauded.

They all have miles to go before their journeys come to an end. No doubt parts of each one's journey will be spent trudging over impossible terrain, but some parts, those that will make the journey worthwhile will — I'm sure, I'm absolutely sure — be spent soaring on the wings of eagles. After all, I had promised them that the truth would set them free.

A year later, when we returned to the same restaurant, this time with over 100 guests, I realised that they were not the only ones who had kept their promises.

I had also kept my promise: the truth had, in fact, set them free.

Epilogue

Of course, it wasn't as easy as the theory of zero-option promise-keeping actually promised. They all kept their promises, but the effort was greater than they had imagined, and the outcomes even more surprising.

The year following the course and leading up to our first reunion was eventful, to say the least.

Margaret, nicknamed by the others 'Queen Bitch', was the most successful financially. She launched herself into an art dealership with an almost addictive passion. The power of the promise at its best, I thought, each time she telephoned me and left me exhausted with her stories of exhibitions, cocktail parties, healthy commissions and exciting encounters with people I had to assume — out of pure ignorance — were art world celebrities.

She had even found a way to differentiate her growing business from other similar businesses. She had hit upon the idea of filming artists discussing the particular work that was on sale and then making that film part of the purchase: she had personalised her business with all the skill of an experienced marketeer. She had also managed to borrow a sizeable sum of money from her father, and by the time the reunion came around she was able to produce an artist's impression (her own) of her art farm.

Her husband Mitch had also moved forward. As he had promised, he went into a private engineering consultancy, not with his intended partner, but with an old fellow graduate who turned up not long after the course ended. I was even more surprised to learn that he was running Margaret's accounts, controlling their joint spending, and making what seemed to me fairly sensible plans for their financial future. He had kept his promise never to gamble again, but in all honesty, I don't think that was particularly difficult for him. But so what? It's not the difficulty of the promise that matters; it's keeping it.

When Grace, with her new boyfriend in tow, turned up at the reunion, very few of us recognised her at first. She was not just thin — she was radiant with health and confidence. I had been concerned about her because I had not heard from her for about six months, but when she walked in I realised she must have been too busy doing more important things. She had, she announced with pride while holding up her promise ring, already completed the first stage in the training required to become a certified fitness instructor. I also learned that she had very little need for my coaching any more. Her boyfriend, the ex-beachball who had been the first to believe in her dream, because he had done the same, had apparently fallen in love with her when she was, to be kind, slightly more than pleasantly plump. They also told me they were both convinced they would make lots of money by conquering the fitness industry. How, exactly, they would do this, they never said. But I wasn't going to puncture their dream by asking.

Surprisingly, I saw more of Andy than of anyone else that year. He became what is sometimes unkindly called a personal development junkie. He read everything, averaged a course a month and sent me e-volumes of mail. Andy was desperate to make a decision, because he had made only one promise: to find out what he really,

really wanted to do in life. Almost every week he changed his mind, but to his credit, he treated his search with the passion and drive it needed.

One day he telephoned me with his discovery. He wanted to do what I do: he wanted to be a lifestyle coach. As soon as he told me, I knew it was right for him; authenticity is obvious when you see it. More importantly, it was achievable. He was my showcase example of someone who had discovered the power of symbol and ritual in promise-keeping, because his promise earring became his most treasured possession.

I remembered how he would talk about the promises he would make, but not make any. He wouldn't make one until he was absolutely sure he would keep it. In fact, he hadn't made a second one yet. He had learned that symbols only work when one transfers power to them. And did he do that! Sometimes listening to him talk about his earring my skin prickled with goosebumps, and for a brief few seconds I would feel as if I was in the presence of a formidable magic. Perhaps I was.

Phil, on the other hand, had been through a particularly difficult year. Trent, his partner, had had to have a few serious operations, and had required much more attention than either of them had anticipated. Consequently, Phil had had to take over Trent's online business and cut down on his taxi shifts. His promise to write 500 words a day no matter what proved quite a challenge. But he did it. 'Half the time I write nonsense,' he told me over the phone one day. 'But I do it. Only 126 days to go. It's become an obsession now.' Not long before the reunion he telephoned me to say that he had found an agent who liked his work. I have yet to learn if he has officially become an author.

Cathy, Phil and Trent ended up the best of friends. Cathy often helped look after Trent, as one would expect from such a generous, beautiful woman. I received a photograph of the three of them dressed in outlandish costumes at an obviously raunchy party. Being just a tad old-fashioned, it was all a bit outrageous for my liking, but her friendship with them paid off, in a manner of speaking. She had started dating someone from Phil's football team, a man she had met on our commitment night. I was not surprised. Her beauty is the sort that keeps poets in work. I also heard, on the grapevine, that her man was quite the business entrepreneur, so if the romance blossoms into spring, Cathy may end up wealthy anyway. I suspect that the thought has not even crossed her mind.

When I go over everything that happened during that year or so, I often think to myself, as the song goes, *what a wonderful world.*

If it's lack of money that's taking the wonder out of your world, I trust you will find a way to bring it back. If it's a feeling that you're not living the life you want, that somehow your dream just keeps fading, I hope you will take my advice and look to the power of the promise.

In my experience, there are few joys comparable to sensing, even briefly, that we can master ourselves by keeping the promises we make. It is in being true to our own word, unconditionally and forever, that we find the power to become truly unstoppable.

As my own teacher once said to me, when I complained about how my own life seemed to be always just more of the same thing, 'Life doesn't stand still, so why should you?'

Why should any of us? Why should I, you, and my wonderful new friends stand still? Why can't we all become unstoppable, particularly now that we know how to?

Do or don't. Bitch or get rich.

The fact that happiness turned out to be as simple as that is, to me, by far the most surprising thing about life.

About the Author

Toney Fitzgerald is an innovator, author, entrepreneur, futurist and successful lifestyle coach to many enthusiastic people around the world. He is the founder and Managing Director of Lifestyle Aspirations Group a specialised lifestyle coaching and education firm.

Toney's personal mission and life purpose is to inspire individuals to aspire to be the best they can be both personally and professionally.

He is known for his pioneering of the personal and professional coaching movement in Australia and New Zealand, starting Coach U, Australia's first school for professional coaches in 1998. In those two years his company trained 250 coaches.

He regularly appears in the press, including *Financial Review*, *The Daily Telegraph*, *The Sunday Telegraph*, *Sydney Morning Herald*, *The Sun Herald*, *The Times* (UK), *New Woman*, as well as on radio and television.

His is also the author of *Start Me Up! – You've got business idea now make it happen* (published by Simon & Schuster).

Please visit our website
www.lifestyleaspirations.com to review:

- Information about our services and products
- Information about seminars, events and appearances by Toney Fitzgerald
- Subscribe to our monthly electronic newsletter

Lifestyle Aspirations Group
PO Box 485 Coogee NSW 2034
Australia
e-mail: info@lifestyleaspirationsgroup.com